Inspirational
Messages
in
Poetry

Inspirational
Messages
in
Poetry

~ For a Deeper Faith ~

Connie Campbell Bratcher

Published by Looking Glass Books
Decatur, Georgia

Scripture quotations from The Holy Bible,
King James Version

Artwork (paintings) by D.D. (Dwight) Watson
Fayetteville, Georgia

Design by Gabriele Ervin
Las Vegas, NV
www.YourImpressions.com

ISBN 1-929619-12-X

Printed in Canada

~ To God Be the Glory ~

Acknowledgments

I would like to express appreciation to the following:

My wonderful son, Barry Bullard, who set up the Internet ministry*, and put many hours of work into this book; my sponsor and loving husband, Ron Bratcher; my precious mother, Betty Campbell; my great pastor, Bill Priester, and church family for all the encouragement and prayers; D.D. Watson, my friend and artist whose paintings appear on the cover and throughout this book as well as on the web site; Gabriele Ervin, my fabulous web designer who also contributed her talents to this book; all who have visited InspirationalPoetry.com and expressed words of encouragement; my publisher, Dick Parker, for his guidance and patience; and most of all, I praise and thank my Lord and Savior, Jesus Christ... without Him, I could do nothing. To God be the Glory!

To you, dear reader, it is the desire of all our hearts that you will be spiritually enriched as you read... "Inspirational Messages in Poetry ~ For a Deeper Faith ~"

Connie Bratcher

*You may view this ministry on the web at either www.InspirationalPoetry.com or www.ChristianPoems.com

Contents

Foreword

Inspirational, moving, instructional, informative, and extremely helpful are some of the words to describe "Inspirational Messages in Poetry." Words of love and hope, whether we write them or receive them, have the remarkable power to transform our state of mind and even alter our emotions through a soul-lifting experience. Probably the most powerful thing about "Inspirational Messages in Poetry," is the fact that it gives to the reader considerable hope for the present, through a deepened faith, which will obviously create a great deal of power for the future.

I challenge you to pick up this special book of poems for a momentary lift in spirit or read them faithfully day by day and let God deepen your faith. You will be blessed and inspired by the words God has given Connie in sharing her faith. What a joy it is to serve as her pastor and watch her faith grow as she serves God continually day by day. Enjoy these poems of faith! This first, in a series of inspirational works by Connie Bratcher, will set the stage for additional writings that will bless our lives and hearts as well. Read them, share them, quote them, and enjoy them; words of inspiration that will deepen our faith and equip us for service.

William O. Priester
Pastor
Flat Creek Baptist Church
Fayetteville, Georgia

Introduction

"Man shall not live by bread alone, but by every word that proceedeth out of the mouth of God." (Matt.4:4)

There is a hunger that can only be satisfied by the Word of God, a thirst that can only be quenched by the Water of Life, our Lord and Savior, Jesus Christ.

This collection of poems was written from a heart that had searched for many years for satisfaction, contentment, peace, and joy. A heart that was hungry and thirsty, but sought fulfillment in things that could not satisfy, only to meet with failure and disappointment. A heart that came to a place of turning to God in total surrender, and found complete satisfaction and fulfillment, as did the prodigal son when he returned home to his father.

"Seek ye first the kingdom of God, and his righteousness; and all these things shall be added unto you." (Matt.6:33).

This world offers much that is appealing to the flesh, but what it offers could never satisfy the deep hunger in the human heart. If God has given you this hunger, the grass will always look greener on the other side of the fence, until you come to the green pastures in the kingdom of God. There you will be completely satisfied. Your loving Shepherd will feed you, and lead you beside the still waters, and you will not only be content within the fold, but you will enjoy the abundant life found only in Him.

"Inspirational Messages in Poetry" can assist you in finding the green pastures where your soul can be fed and your thirst quenched.

Jesus said: "Blessed are they which do hunger and thirst after righteousness: for they shall be filled." (Matt. 5:6).

Faith Messages I

"For God so loved the world,
that he gave his only begotten Son,
that whosoever believeth in him should not perish,
but have everlasting life."
(John 3:16)

Faith I

The Old Rugged Cross

True Liberty

The Christ

Beauty

The Saviour

Seek and You Shall Find

Just as We Are

Payment In Full

A New Creation

Justified by Faith

What a Difference

Called into Light

Holy Light

Peace

He's Always There

Follow the Master

So Many Blessings

It Would Cause Us to Shout

All Within His Plan

God's Grace Is Sufficient

The Valley Times

Where Souls Draw Nigh

In God's Time

Rejoice Evermore

The Right Path

Life

The Prize

Our Life's Message

Unworthy

Everyone Is Special

Temptation

In His Loving Arms

We're All Human

Forgive

An Unspoken Language

Misery

On the Giving Side

Only One

Time

Right Where We Live

His Schedule

God's Computer

God's Recorder

Heavenly Band

Where Is Home

We Shall See Him

Well Done

What Lies Ahead

Contentment

What Greater Love?

TRUE LIBERTY

Christ, our shining Light – The Son of God above,
Calls out to one and all, proclaiming the Father's love:
"Come ye who are tired and weary,
Those who are tempest tossed;
The homeless, hungry, poor,
The wretched, sinful lost;
Come all ye huddled masses yearning to be free;
From a weary world of darkness, come ye unto me.
My yoke is easy, my burden light,
There's rest on the peaceful shore,
I lift my lamp eternally beside the golden door."

"If the Son therefore shall make you free,
ye shall be free indeed."
(John 8:36)

Inspired by "The New Colossus", a poem by Emma Lazarus
inscribed on a tablet in the pedestal of the
Statue of Liberty in 1903.

THE CHRIST

"Thou art the Christ, the Son of the living God,"
Peter answered our Lord one day;
And upon this truth, God builds His church
On the straight and narrow way.
The Christ who shed His precious blood
On the cross of Calvary
Could have called a host of angels,
But chose to die for you and me.
The Christ who arose victoriously
Over sin, death and the grave,
Extends His Hand of mercy,
Our sinful souls to save.
Lifted in a world of darkness
For all mankind to see...
Those who bow before Him
Shall live eternally.

"And I, if I be lifted up from the earth,
will draw all men unto me."
(John 12:32)

BEAUTY

God and His works are wondrous indeed –
He has given so freely to meet every need.
Creator of all, and such beauty about,
The sunrise alone would cause one to shout;
And what can compare with the beauty of a rose,
Or a stream on the mountain as gently it flows?
Such beauty there is in the heavens above,
With the moon and stars proclaiming God's love;
And lovelier still, the embrace of a friend,
Expressing the purity of love within –
But the Greatest of all beauties God wants us to see,
Is the Gift of his Son on Mount Calvary.

"For God so loved the world,
that he gave his only begotten Son,
that whosoever believeth in him should not perish,
but have everlasting life."
(John 3:16)

THE SAVIOUR

He left the glory of heaven and by a miraculous birth,
God's only Son came to walk upon earth.
He came unto His own, and they knew Him not,
The lamb of God, without blemish or spot.
He healed the sick, raised the dead,
And with a little lunch, the multitude fed.
He made the deaf to hear, the blind to see,
Cast out demons and set men free.
Then He was nailed upon an old rugged tree
To pay the debt for you and me.
They placed Him in a tomb, sealed it tight,
Guarded it well both day and night...
But, the tomb could not hold Him – Hallelujah!...
He Arose!...
The Victor over sin, death, the grave and all foes.
Glory to God, He's a living King.
He takes a sorrowful heart and makes it sing.
He takes a sin sick soul filled with misery and strife,
And by His grace imparts a brand new life.
It's the miracle of all miracles when He saves a soul,
Praise His Name – He makes us whole.

"He came unto his own, and they received him not,
but as many as received him
to them gave he power to become the sons of God."
(John 1:11-12)

SEEK AND YOU SHALL FIND

"Ask and it shall be given unto you,
Seek and you shall find."
As you submit to Christ in all you do,
He'll cleanse your heart and mind –
Satisfying your hungry soul each day
With manna from above,
Revealing to you His will and way,
And His unchanging love.
"Knock and it shall be opened unto you" –
God's grace and power receive.
He'll give you joy and life anew,
And all your fears relieve.
As you stand on firm foundation –
Christ, the solid Rock,
There's assurance of salvation,
And blessings when you knock.
So, "Ask and it shall be given unto you,
Seek and you shall find."
His peace will, surely flood your soul,
And heal your troubled mind.

"He is a rewarder of them that diligently seek him."
(Heb. 11:6)

JUST AS WE ARE

Just as we are – without one plea –
Bound by sin's captivity;
Convicted and broken, we bend our knee
To the One who died to set us free.
Turmoil and strife shall all depart,
As He touches and heals our shattered heart.
The wars and fears within shall cease,
Replaced with abundant joy and peace.
Yes, just as we are – not a single plea,
At the foot of the Cross, He sets us free.
At last our blinded eyes can see,
As we're born anew for eternity –
A miracle wrought by God's own hand;
From time of creation, it was in His plan.
Thank You, Father, for Your grace from afar
That touches our souls – Just As We Are.

"But God commendeth his love toward us,
in that, while we were yet sinners,
Christ died for us."
(Rom. 5:8)

PAYMENT IN FULL

Bought with a price, no longer my own –
Such a wonderful life, as never I've known.
The shed blood of Christ made me whole –
Now I am His, a sheep in the fold.
Filled with joy unspeakable and full of glory;
Reaching out to others with the old, old story
Of that rugged cross where He paid for our sin,
That we might be delivered and cleansed within.
Though bought with a price as a slave would be,
As new creatures in Him, we are set free –
Free to live a Godly life,
Given power over sin and strife,
Enabled to walk in the Spirit each day,
As we travel along life's narrow way.
Yes, a bond servant to Christ, yet totally free –
Salvation by grace, a great mystery.
Repent and believe, surrendering your all,
As you respond on your knees to the Master's call.
This is all God requires you to do –
Payment In Full has been made for you.

"For ye are bought with a price;
therefore glorify God in your body
and in your spirit; which are God's."
(I Cor. 6:20)

A NEW CREATION

"If anyone's in Christ, all things are made new;"
Not many find Him, only a few.
He's the only way to eternal life,
And freedom from all sin and strife.
As we bow before Him repenting of sin,
His Holy Spirit comes to live within –
Forgiving us, and setting us free
To live for Him as was meant to be.
He directs our paths as we walk each day,
And promises to be with us all the way.
Thank you, Father, for loving us so;
And for abundant life that we can know,
When we surrender our all,
In response to Your call.
Thank You for Christ who died for our sin;
Use us, we pray, some soul to win.

"Therefore if any man be in Christ,
he is a new creature:
old things are passed away; behold,
all things are become new."
(II Cor. 5:17)

JUSTIFIED BY FAITH

Justified by Faith, cleansed and made whole,
Forgiven by God, now a satisfied soul.
Led by His Spirit the righteous way,
Fed by His Word, never to stray.
Filled with His goodness, grace and love
Imparted by the heavenly Father above.
Given freedom from darkness, sin and strife,
Justified by Faith – a brand new life.

"Therefore being Justified by faith,
we have peace with God
through our Lord Jesus Christ."
(Rom. 5:1)

WHAT A DIFFERENCE

What a difference it makes when in total despair,
One cries out to God while kneeling in prayer,
And God's divine power comes down from above,
Filling the heart with peace and love.
What a difference there is when one goes astray,
And calls upon the Father to show him the way –
Then God in His mercy reveals His own son,
It's through His shed blood the battle is won.
What a difference there is when one lost in sin
Bows in repentance, and Jesus comes in.
That soul now lives as never before,
And shall dwell with God forevermore.
What a difference it makes... Praise His holy name!
When God touches something, it's never the same.

"Even when we were dead in sins,
God quickened us together with Christ,
and hath raised us up together,
and made us sit together in
heavenly places in Christ Jesus."
(Eph. 2:5-6)

CALLED INTO LIGHT

We're called from darkness into God's marvelous light,
To show forth His praises to those without sight –
Spiritually blinded because of sin,
In need of the Master's touch within.
We rejoice in the salvation of our own soul,
Brought from darkness Into His fold;
Then we think of those who've never heard
The gospel of Christ and His precious word,
And our heart cries out, "Lord, use me I pray,
To make Your message known today.
May Your light, somehow, shine forth through me
To open blinded eyes that they may see,
And be delivered from the state of darkness and sin,
As they enter Your kingdom of light within.
Just as You cleansed the leper and healed the lame,
When You give spiritual sight the miracle's the same.
So thank You, Lord, that we're Called Into Light
By Your miracle working Power that gives us sight."

"Ye should show forth the praises of
him who hath called you
out of darkness into his marvellous light."
(I Peter 2:9)

HOLY LIGHT

To see a sparkling little beam
In a star that shines so bright,
We catch a tiny glory stream
As we worship by it's light –
A glimpse of our home on high,
Where we'll meet Him face to face –
Beyond the beautiful starlit sky,
We'll enter by His grace.
No more just a little beam
Sparkling from a star;
Nor just a tiny glory stream
In that heavenly place afar;
But surrounded by God's glory bright,
Forever with Him we'll be;
There to bask in Holy Light –
As we worship eternally.

"… no need of the sun, neither of the moon, to shine in it:
for the glory of God did lighten it,
and the Lamb is the light thereof."
(Rev. 21:23)

PEACE

He calmed the angry storm simply saying, "Peace be still."
The wind and sea obey Him bowing at His will.
As we turn our eyes on Jesus, submitting to His call,
His Spirit calms our troubled heart,
Giving peace whate'er befall.
What blissful sweet communion
With our heavenly Father above,
As we become partakers of His goodness, grace and love.
He bestows upon His people all heavenly fruits to bear,
While keeping them safely sheltered in His tender loving care.
How could we cease to praise the One who satisfies our heart,
Removing the sin and turmoil, sweet peace to impart.
It passes all understanding, this fruit of the heavenly Dove,
And is free to all who come to Him
Seeking mercy, truth and love.
Yes, our Lord is ready to quiet the storm,
And calm the troubled sea
Of those who bow before Him in faith and humility.
Knowing He's in complete control,
All fears within shall cease –
Be still and know that He is God...
He'll give you perfect Peace.

"Peace I leave with you, my peace I give unto you."
(John 14:27)

HE'S ALWAYS THERE

It matters not what path we take,
The high road or the low,
Our heavenly Father is always there
Wherever we may go.
Whatever turn we make in life –
To the left or to the right,
However far we venture out,
We're still within His sight.
If we ascend into the heavens,
There our Lord will be.
If we make our bed in hell,
His grieving Heart shall see.
His eye is on the sparrow,
He takes note if it should fall;
And how much more He cares for us
Who respond to His gentle call.
Under His Wings we're sheltered,
While held within His Hand;
His grace and power enabling us
Temptation to withstand.
A friend closer than a brother,
Our burdens all to bear –
Such a tender, loving Shepherd,
Yes, "He's Always There."

"Whither shall I go from thy Spirit? or
whither shall I flee from thy presence?"
(Ps. 139:7)

FOLLOW THE MASTER

Take not the wrong road, which is easy to do,
But follow the Master who's righteous and true.
Be not overcome by loneliness and fear,
The loving Master is ever so near.
When you're troubled by this world's affairs,
Look to the Master – the One who cares;
And never be discouraged by the meanness about,
Just trust in the Master, forsaking all doubt.
Take no anxious thought about what lies ahead –
For He who holds the future is alive from the dead,
Ready to lead in the righteous way...
Those who will follow Him day by day.
Praise His name, what a great God is He....
Jesus the Master, through eternity.

"If any man will come after me,
let him take up his cross,
and follow me."
(Matt. 16:24)

So Many Blessings

There are so many blessings in this life,
How thankful we should be.
The sunrise, sunset, the mountains and streams,
Such magnificent sights to see –
Springtime splendor, the flowers in bloom,
The moon and stars at night,
Gloriously beaming down on us,
Shining their light so bright...
So many blessings flood our souls
Causing our hearts to shout,
Simple things we see each day
That some never think about.
There's the countryside with cattle on the hills,
Peacefully feeding their young,
And the songbirds singing such melodies
Like never before heard sung.
To watch them diligently building their nest,
As each plays its own part,
Then seeing them care for the baby birds
Truly touches the heart.
Such wonderful blessings indeed,
In heaven and earth surround;
We can see them in our family and friends,
If we'll just look around.
Let us always count our blessings,
Naming them one by one.

Then with thankful hearts we'll worship God,
And praise Him for all He's done.
Yes, so many blessings along life's way,
And every one of them free;
Thank You, Lord, for giving to us
The spiritual eyes to see.

"Blessed be the God and Father of our Lord
Jesus Christ, who hath blessed us with all
spiritual blessings in heavenly places in Christ."
(Eph. 1:3)

IT WOULD CAUSE US TO SHOUT

It would cause us to shout, that city to behold,
Where God's glory shines forth from the streets of pure gold.
Such a great reunion – friends and loved ones to see,
Heartaches all vanished, at last to be free.
Yes, it would cause us to shout – that home on high,
Prepared for us beyond the sky.
The songs of angels without cease –
A state of perfect harmony and peace.
Oh, how we'll shout when we see His face,
And hear Him proclaim, "you have run a good race."
But, what about the blessings He's given today?
In grace and love He's shown us the way.
He's brought us from death into life anew;
Such compassion He had for me and for you.
His death on the cross was love indeed,
And He lives today to meet every need.
So, why worry, why fret or have any doubt?
A Saviour like this should cause us to shout!!!

"Shout unto God with the voice of triumph."
(Ps. 47:1)

ALL WITHIN HIS PLAN

Sometimes things happen we don't understand
And we begin to question why...
Heartache, pain, disappointment and sorrow
Just do not pass us by.
Even though we're committed to God,
And led by His own hand,
Trouble and trials still come our way,
And it's all within His plan.
Our Saviour Himself faced hardship on earth,
As He was tempted, tested and tried.
He suffered great pain and agony,
And on the old rugged cross He died.
But He arose victorious over sin,
Death and the grave,
And He lives forever –
Our souls to save.
So, when troublesome times come
And we have burdens to bear,
Let us always remember our Lord is there,
To comfort, strengthen, and be our guide,
As we follow His word,
And in Him abide....
And where we can't trace Him
In what comes our way,
Let us simply trust Him
As we walk each day,
Knowing He's fully in control,
Working all things out
For the good of our soul.
Then as we're tempted to question why...
When things happen we don't understand,
Let us on Him completely rely,
Knowing all is within His plan.

"According to the eternal purpose which he purposed
in Christ Jesus our Lord."
(Eph. 3:11)

27

GOD'S GRACE IS SUFFICIENT

In God's Holy written Word we read,
His grace is sufficient to meet every need.
How clear this truth is brought into view,
When trials come, and so often they do.
It's in these times, to Him we flee,
Bowing in submission, on bended knee.
We then become His softened clay,
Ready for molding, as humbly we pray.
Heartache, tragedy, disappointment, and pain,
Are the Potter's tools for our spiritual gain.
Whatever hardships we encounter each day
Only conform us to His will and way.
Our Lord walks with us, as we go through it all,
Many times carrying us, lest we should fall;
And that truth which we simply believed before,
Now comes into focus even more;
For the written words on the pages we see
Have truly become a reality –
And we know more fully what it's all about...
God's Grace Is Sufficient without a doubt !!!

"My grace is sufficient for thee;
for my strength is made perfect in weakness."
(II Cor. 12:9)

THE VALLEY TIMES

The depth of the valley we dread so much
Enables us to know God's special touch.
Heartache, suffering, loneliness, and fear
All are made bearable as we feel Him near.
With tender compassion He carries us through,
Teaching, comforting, revealing what's true.
It's in these valley times we're made ready to mold –
Resting in His hands – we come forth as pure gold.
So, thank you, Father, for the valley's each day
That conform us to Christ, and Your holy way.

"It is good for me that I have been afflicted;
that I might learn they statues."
(Ps. 119:71)

WHERE SOULS DRAW NIGH

In the darkest night there shines a light,
And all who look shall see,
The radiant glow that fills the soul,
And sets the captive free.
In the deepest valley there's a mountain peak
For all to gaze upon.
It lifts the spirit, giving grace and hope,
Until the battle's won.
In sickness there's a great physician
Whose touch can make us whole,
And all who come to Him for healing
Are cleansed within the soul.
In sorrow there's a comforter
Who loves beyond compare.
He's touched with our infirmities,
Our burdens all to bear.
In poverty there's abundant wealth
That this world cannot measure.
No one there goes hungry,
Who feeds on heavenly treasure.
Thank God for the Light in darkness,
And for the mountain high.
Thank Him for the valley deep,
Where Souls to Him Draw Nigh.

"Draw nigh to God, and he will draw nigh to you."
(James 4:8)

IN GOD'S TIME

A baby is conceived and comes to earth... in God's time
A seeking soul finds spiritual birth... in God's time
Flowers bloom so beautifully in spring.. .in God's time
The birds build their nest as they sing... in God's time
We feel the evening breeze softly blow... in God's time
And assurance is given that He loves us so... in His time
Yet, when troublesome times come and skies are gray,
Too often we complain.
A man named Job did this one day,
And his life was never the same –
Until he awakened and began to see,
It was working for his own good.
He bowed his knee and finally
At last he understood...
Shall we accept good and not the bad?
The happy times and not the sad?
All things are from God's own hand,
And are working according to His plan... In His time
So, when the storms of life linger
With dark clouds all about,
Let us look to our Saviour
Knowing the sun will come out... In His Time
Let us trust Him whatever comes our way –
His grace is sufficient for us each day.
Then we'll understand fully as time goes by,
When one day we enter the kingdom on high... In God's Time.

"To everything there is a season,
and a time to every purpose under the heaven."
(Ec. 3:1)

REJOICE EVERMORE

Where is joy unspeakable and full of glory?
Where is the rejoicing in that old, old story?
How it must grieve God's Spirit today
To see his children so far astray –
Looking to circumstances rather than Him;
Striving and fighting at every whim...
Hearts filled with hatred, judgment and sin,
Not willing to bow for cleansing within.
Repentance is needed where there's doom and gloom,
For such in God's kingdom, there just isn't room.
Christ came to give abundant life –
Giving joy and peace in place of strife.
He fights the battle for us as we walk and pray,
Giving the victory day by day.
Oh, glory to God, praise His Holy Name,
Our gracious God is ever the same –
Ready to forgive, to cleanse and make whole,
Bringing lost sinners into his fold.
So, why should we fret or fear things to come,
Or be heavy ladened and weary as some?
Let us come unto Christ and He'll give us rest,
Richly blessing us with His very best.
Lord, deliver us from oppression I pray,
And may we follow only Thee each day.

Lead us in the paths that we should take,
That we might truly serve thee for Thy name's sake;
And may we obey this clear command
Given in scripture by Thine own hand:
"If there be any virtue, if there be any praise,
Think on these things" and "Rejoice Evermore."

"For our heart shall rejoice in him,
because we have trusted in his holy name."
(Ps. 33:21)

THE RIGHT PATH

Suppose we had chosen another path
Other than the one we're on –
Would we be happier and more content,
Or would we be sad and alone?
Life's choices are difficult when we're young;
There are so many ways to go.
Our human eyes can't see ahead,
So how are we to know?
We make decisions, both good and bad
As we live our lives each day –
Then wonder what we would have had,
If we'd chosen another way.
Like helpless sheep we wander,
Needing the Shepherd by our side.
The one who knows what lies ahead
Reaches out to be our guide.
Whatever path that we are on
Is where we need to be;
For our Lord meets us where we are,
And there He sets us free
To experience joy and all life's best
Within His loving fold.
Our hearts then are truly blessed
With peace that fills the soul.
So, when we begin to question "if"...
As we look back long ago,

Let us keep one thing in mind
That's important for us to know...
"Whatever might have been
Is never as good as what is,
For the choices we make, apart from God,
Are never as good as His"...
So, let us surrender to His control
as we walk with Him each day –
Then we can rest assured
We're on The Right Path
Never to wander away.

"Ponder the path of thy feet,
and let all thy ways be established."
(Prov. 4:26)

LIFE

Life is given by the Creator above –
A precious gift of His great love;
To be valued, protected, kept safe and sound,
A wonderful treasure wherever it's found.
God loves His creatures, both great and small –
It grieves His heart for a sparrow to fall;
And how much more He loves you and me –
The proof is found on Mount Calvary.
What He did for us there was in His plan –
Our Lord gave his life to redeem fallen man.
Having paid such a price for our spiritual birth,
He revealed so clearly our life's worth.
We're valuable to God, it's plain to see.
He sacrificed His Son to set us free.
As we bow before Him, we're abundantly blessed,
Forgiven and cleansed, as our sin is confessed.
Through repentance and faith we're born again,
Brought into God's kingdom by His own hand.
Such peace and joy with His Spirit within,
Giving us the victory over sin.
We now have life as never before,
In the heavenly kingdom forevermore.
Thank you, Lord, for loving us so;
May we reach out that others may know
This spiritual life, so abundant and free.
Open their eyes, Lord, that they may see –
Life is so precious, and comes from Thee.

"The Spirit of God hath made me;
and the breath of the Almighty hath given me life."
(Job 33:4)

THE PRIZE

We dream our dreams and plan our plans,
Then work to meet our goals.
Failure and stress along the way
Take their toll upon our souls;
But it's worth it all in light of the prize
We see gleaming at the end...
Satisfaction, happiness and joy await...
Just around the bend.
Time passes, oh, so swiftly,
As we travel toward the goal,
And our sight becomes much clearer
As the body's growing old –
For the prize shines much more brightly
Than it ever did before –
Having reached the goal we find it...
At our own front door.
Not just waiting round the bend,
The prize we sought is found within.
So let's dream our dreams and plan our plans,
And work to meet our goals...
Enjoying the prize along the way
That lies within our souls.

"The kingdom of God is within you."
(Luke 17:21)

OUR LIFE'S MESSAGE

Our life is like a flower, from a little seed it grows.
Whatever will become of it, no human ever knows.
It's fed and nurtured, given love and care;
Then as it blossoms, we're suddenly aware
Of just what that life was meant to be,
For it now is made plain for all to see.
Yes, our life is a message that others will read,
And hopefully what's read will meet some need.
So may our morals be high and our character strong,
Doing what's right and avoiding all wrong,
For the time is short, it's fleeting by,
And like a flower, we fade and die –
But the message we leave for all to see,
Shall remain forever, through eternity.

"Let your light shine before men,
that they may see your good works,
and glorify your Father which is in heaven."
(Matt. 5:16)

UNWORTHY

Unworthy of that wondrous love bestowed upon my heart
By Him who suffered, bled and died, salvation to impart.
Unworthy of such marvelous grace brought down to lowly man;
Free to all whom He would call, redemption's in His hand.
Unworthy of that walk with Him, such fellowship divine;
What heavenly bliss to know Him,
His Spirit communing with mine.
Unworthy of that chastening rod, as I would go astray,
Conveying again the Father's love, bringing me back into his way.
Unworthy of the peace and joy, our God alone imparts,
That satisfies the emptiness within our lonely hearts.
Unworthy, yes unworthy still, though children of the King we are –
Giving honor, praise and glory to Him for that one sent from afar.
He gave up His life that we might live to glorify His name –
From an unworthy sinner to an unworthy saint,
The message is still the same.
Unworthy of His forgiving power and of His tender care...
Oh, glorious day when we see His face,
And bow at His feet o'er there.
Keep us at the foot of the cross, oh, Shepherd of my soul –
That no flesh would glory in thy presence,
But this truth would sure unfold...
"Unworthy"

"That no flesh should glory in his presence."
(I Cor. 1:29)

EVERYONE IS SPECIAL

Everyone Is Special in his own way,
Each having his own part to play;
Yet, it's not like acting out some role –
Real life effects the heart and soul;
And how important it is for us to be
Preparing ourselves for eternity,
By making sure that the part we play
Brings glory and honor to God each day.
He made one of a kind – each is unique –
The way we look, and the way we speak.
We have a gift that's all our own,
Belonging to only us alone,
Freely given by the Father above
For the purpose of sharing His great love.
So, why compare ourselves with our brother?
Everyone Is Special, none like another;
And let us not just act out our part,
Whatever we do should come from the heart.
May we be ourselves – honest and true,
For there's only one me, and only one you.

"Glorify God in your body,
and in your Spirit which are God's."
(I Cor. 6:20)

TEMPTATION

Satan comes as an angel of light,
With glittering pleasures untold;
And many hearts are led astray,
Far from the peaceful fold.
He knows our point of weakness,
Just how to lure us all...
Till fellowship with God is broken,
And we yield to him and fall.
Those pleasures so enticing
Were short lived, as we'd been told;
And the angel of light that deceived us
Was a lion, fierce and bold,
Leaving us bruised and bleeding
In need of tender care...
We cry to our loving Shepherd
And find He's always there.
Satan is a defeated foe,
Conquered at the Cross;
We need not yield to him at all
And suffer such a loss.
As we walk in fellowship with God,
From sin He set's us free,
Giving power o'er the tempter's call...
Resist him... he will flee.

"Submit yourselves therefore to God,
resist the devil, and he will flee from you."
(James 4:7)

IN HIS LOVING ARMS

God holds us in His loving arms,
Shielding us from the tempter's charms;
Teaching us to deny worldly lusts,
As we yield to Him, and fully trust.
In His mighty arms we rest,
Troubled on every side,
Yet not distressed;
Perplexed, but not in despair,
For we're safely sheltered
In His tender care.
Persecuted, but not forsaken,
Though the foundations
all around are shaken.
Our Lord protects us
From all alarms,
As He holds us securely
In His Loving Arms.

"For Thou hast been a shelter for me,
and a strong tower from the enemy."
(Ps. 61:3)

WE'RE ALL HUMAN

Not one of us is perfect, it's plain to see,
Although we all would like to be.
We make mistakes and even sin,
And then when caught, our actions defend.
We see others do the same as we look about;
We're all so human, without a doubt.
So, may we never think of ourselves better than a brother;
For we're all on the same level with one another...
In need of God's touch from above,
Filling our hearts with his great love.
Whenever we see someone stumble and fall,
Let us never come down on them at all,
But point them to the Saviour who meets our need,
Ready and willing our soul to feed.
Lord, you're the only one who's perfect or ever will be,
And it's through your power that we're set free.
So, help us to be kind and not criticize,
But always see others through your eyes,
As we look beyond their weakness and sin,
To what they can be with your Spirit within.
Thank you, Lord, that we who are human can be made whole –
As you reach out in mercy and save our soul.

"For all have sinned, and come
short of the glory of God."
(Rom. 3:23)

FORGIVE

"Forgive and it shall be forgiven you",
Instructions by God's own Son.
Whatever wrongs someone may do,
We're to forgive them every one.
When someone offends us, treating us bad,
We tend to flare up and fight;
But as we look back at times we've had,
When we weren't living right;
Then we see our wrongs and our own sin,
As we've stumbled along life's way.
How many times have we hurt a friend,
And we still slip and fall today.
So, when we see the sins of our brother,
Surely no stones can we cast;
For how can we not forgive one another
When God has forgiven our past?
May we forgive as we've been forgiven,
"Seventy times seven a day"–
Then our hearts will be in tune with heaven
As God leads us on our way.

"Be ye kind one to another, tenderhearted, forgiving one another,
even as God for Christ's sake has forgiven you."
(Eph. 4:32)

AN UNSPOKEN LANGUAGE

The tender touch of a loving hand
Is an unspoken language we all understand.
A gentle embrace in time of need
Sends an unwritten message all can read.
A warm smile cost nothing to give
And touches our hearts right where we live.
If all knew this language so beautiful and pure,
Our world would be a better place for sure.
It comes from our heavenly Father above...
An Unspoken Language... The language of love.

"Love one another; as I have loved you –
by this shall all men know that ye are my disciples."
(John 13:34-35)

45

MISERY

If you want to be miserable and really feel low,
Focus your thoughts on all of your woe.
Think of your troubles, heartaches and pain;
Never the sunshine, only the rain.
Think of the awfulness of yesterday,
How others mistreated you along the way.
Then the opportunities that passed you by;
The failures you encountered each time you'd try.
Think of the tragedy that might happen some day;
Never the blue skies, only the gray –
But regardless of whatever else you may do,
Just think of yourself... and only of you.

"Look not every man on his own things,
but every man also on
the things of others."
(Phil. 2:4)

ON THE GIVING SIDE

How wonderful to receive a gift from a friend.
It always stirs a warm feeling within;
And as happy as we are with the gift,
It's the thought behind it that gives us the lift,
Making us so very keenly aware
There still are those who truly care.
But a more wonderful thing, I must confide,
Is when we are on the giving side.
Nothing compares with what comes our way,
As we reach out a hand to others each day.
"Give and it shall be given unto you"...
This verse in God's word is surely true.
He blesses us richly as we reach out,
Teaching us what giving is all about,
And we find it's not hard at all to believe,
"It's better to give than it is to receive."
Lord, as we live each day and in you abide,
Keep us, I pray, on the giving side.

"Freely ye have received, freely give."
(Matt. 10:8)

ONLY ONE

Suppose those things you'd like to see changed
All depended on you.
Would you be willing to meet the task
Doing all that you could do?
We need only to open our eyes to see
A world full of trouble and cares.
Would any needs at all be met
If it depended on only our prayers?
How often we say, "I'll pray for you,"
And merrily on we go,
Never giving a thought to the need again
And the one who's hurting so.
Lord, forgive us of our complacency
When we're neither hot nor cold –
For our selfishness and passivity
In the security of your fold.
How your heart must truly grieve
To see us wander away;
So much from your hand we receive
As we look to you each day.
Blessings too many to number
You've bestowed upon our souls-
Awaken us, we pray, from slumber
To work within the fold.
"To whom much is given, much is required" –
May the needs not be left to our brother,
But help us reach out as we're inspired
To meet the needs of another,
And work heartily until the task is done...
As though it depended on Only One.

"And whatsoever ye do, do it heartily,
as to the Lord, and not unto men."
(Col. 3:23)

TIME

So precious is time, yet we squander it away,
Unaware of it's value, we drift through the day.
So precious is time, yet what have we to show
For the years gone by, and so swiftly they go.
Where are the fruits of yesterday?
What has been accomplished along life's way?
Oh hasten brother, sister too,
Hasten today, God's will to do.
An hour lost is gone forever;
A moment is wasted to return... never.
We may not understand it all, nor his face clearly see,
But let us labor moment by moment for the things of eternity;
And though at times we be discouraged,
May we never be cast down...
But endure as soldiers of the cross,
Till that last sheep be found.
With God's word as our sword, we'll march on to victory,
Going out in his name to set men free.
Oh God, help us to know all else is sinking sand,
And may we redeem the time, for thy kingdom is at hand.

"See then that ye walk circumspectly,
not as fools, but as wise,
redeeming the time, because the days are evil."
(Eph. 5:15-16)

RIGHT WHERE WE LIVE

Grieving souls need comfort and care.
Those who are lonely need someone there.
The broken hearted could use a friend
To lean on as they heal and mend.
Little children need lots of love,
And training in the ways of the Father above.
Souls that are searching need to know the way
To our Lord and Saviour who lives today...
Ready to forgive and set men free,
Regardless of what their sins may be.
So many needs in our world around,
Help us, Lord, to always be found
Reaching out, a helping hand to give...
Making a difference Right Where We Live.

"In as much as ye have done it unto
one of the least of these my brethren,
ye have done it unto me."
(Matt. 25:40)

HIS SCHEDULE

So little time and so much to do –
Sometimes we're in a dither.
We wring our hands and fuss, it's true,
Then our Lord calls us – "Come hither."
As we come to Him, He gives us rest
Within our weary soul,
And we realize we do our best
When surrendered to His control.
He knows the beginning from the end
And just what lies ahead.
Our anxious heart He'll take and mend,
Giving peace and joy instead.
So, when we feel there's so little time,
And just too much to do,
Let us remember who's schedule we're on,
He'll always see us through.
He may make changes as we go along…
Removing some things that don't belong,
Correcting our priorities,
Adding a few simplicities;
For "His ways are not our ways," we are told,
And He knows what's best for our soul.
So, let us follow His Schedule each day,
and trust Him to work in His perfect way.

"The steps of a good man are ordered by the Lord:
and he delighteth in his way."
(Ps. 37:23)

GOD'S COMPUTER

God's computer, by His own design –
As we come to Christ, we're plugged into His line.
Qualified by grace to tap into His power,
Activating our lives for the need of the hour.
Made the programmer of our own soul,
Yet His computer, under His control.
His word is the software needed to function,
By his Holy Spirit we're given the unction.
As we feed the scriptures into our heart,
Allowing God to cleanse every part,
The computer becomes valuable in the Master's hand –
Communicating truth throughout the land.
Our system needs booting when we go astray,
So, we shut off the computer, and kneel to pray.
The creator knows all about the trouble that's there,
And as we turn to Him, He's ready to repair.
The errors are removed, the power turned on,
A tool once again, His message to make known.
We program more carefully as we go our way,
Feeding in the right data from day to day...
An information channel to reach far and wide –
Oh, to be God's computer, as in Him we abide.

"If a man purge himself from iniquity, he shall be a vessel
unto honor, sanctified, and meet for the master's use,
and prepared unto every good work."
(II Tim. 2:21)

GOD'S RECORDER

God's recorder is hidden from view
Recording the things we say and do.
We'll give an account to Him one day
For what we do and what we say.
Thoughts and intentions are recorded as well –
Things we may or may not tell;
All are taped on the Master's machine
To be viewed and judged on His heavenly screen.
Under conviction we see our soul within,
Apart from God and lost in sin;
Then confessing we repent, on bended knee,
To the one who died to set us free.
The tape is reversed to the very start...
God erases it all as he cleanses our heart.
A new beginning by his marvelous grace,
Equipping us fully, temptation to face.
No longer yielding to this world's charms,
We rest completely in our Savior's arms.
At times we slip and fall short of His best,
Failing to meet the trial or the test –
Again we come to our Lord in prayer,
And asking forgiveness, we find Him there,
Ready to cleanse as we seek His face –
Yes, our loving Father once again will erase...
Removing that which doesn't belong,
Replacing it with a joyful song.
Oh, may our lives be found in decent order...
When our tape is played by God's Recorder.

"If we confess our sins, he is faithful and just to forgive us our sins,
and to cleanse us from all unrighteousness."
(I John 1:9)

HEAVENLY BAND

A musical instrument must be tuned
To play at it's very best,
And our hearts must be in tune with God
To enjoy a life that's blessed.
The strings are undone, torn and tattered,
Having lived for self alone.
Eternal things that really mattered
Were never even known.
Then the Master musician takes our broken heart
Into His skillful hand,
Cleansing, preparing, renewing it,
For His glorious heavenly band.
The strings are replaced with ones of pure gold,
Fine tuned by the Shepherd of His fold.
A beautiful rhapsody now can be heard,
Like the melody of a joyful, sweet song bird –
A blessing to all who hear and see,
The music that sets the captive free...
Now an instrument made ready for the finest sound,
In perfect harmony and heavenward bound –
Solid and secure in the Master's hand...
Forever to be in His Heavenly Band.

"I give to them eternal life; and they shall never perish,
neither shall any man pluck them out of my hand."
(John 10:28)

WHERE IS HOME?

"Home is where the heart is,"
We've so often heard it told,
But as we think more carefully,
Some other thoughts unfold.
We give our hearts to many things
As we live our lives each day –
Vain, meaningless, worldly things,
For we tend to wander away
From our God who wants the best for us,
And meets our every need.
When we turn our eyes away from Him,
His word we cease to heed.
Then our hearts are deceitful and have gone astray,
In need of the Master's touch.
Lord, bring us back to Thee I pray,
For we need you so much.
Our home is with our Saviour,
And it's there that peace is found;
So, may our "heart be where the Home is" –
And not the other way around.

"The heart is deceitful above all things."
(Jer. 17:9)

WE SHALL SEE HIM

We've never seen God with the visible eye,
But to know He exists just look at the sky...
The sunrise and sunset, so colorfully bright,
The moon and the stars, as they glisten by night –
His handiwork is seen in the sea and on land;
Such majestic splendor by His own hand.
How could we ever begin to doubt,
With these glorious sights as we look about.
Our God is real, it's plain to see,
And He reaches down our guide to be,
Keeping us on the narrow way,
As we humbly walk with Him each day.
He is the Shepherd of our soul,
Throughout our life, both young and old,
And at the end we can surely say –
Our God was with us all the way,
Guiding us into his glory above
To live forever in His great love.
The beauty of His face we then shall see,
As we dwell with Him through eternity.

"Now we see through a glass, darkly;
but then face to face."
(I Cor. 13:12)

WELL DONE

Oh, to hear those words when we see His face,
At the end of time in that glorious place.
We'll bow before Him, worshipping our King,
As we hear the host of angels sing.
A crown of righteousness awaits, we're told,
For our faithfulness within the fold;
But at His feet our crown we'll cast,
When our wonderful Saviour we meet at last.
Yes, face to face we'll see Him there,
The one who died, our sins to bear.
He made the way for our spiritual birth,
And abundant life upon the earth.
As we enter into glory with our merciful King,
Along with the angels we'll eternally sing...
Praises to His name for His marvelous grace,
Enabling us to enter His Holy Place –
And as faithful servants who've received God's Son,
We'll hear his voice say to us... "Well Done."

"His Lord said unto him, well done
thou good and faithful servant."
(Matt. 25:21)

WHAT LIES AHEAD

The exact state of eternity
Is not for you and me to see;
For we do not know what lies ahead,
Only what our Lord has said.
It's through a glass darkly we look while here,
But then face to face, all will be clear.
He said there are mansions with streets of pure gold,
And angels singing as blessings unfold –
A glorious state of harmony and peace,
Joyful bliss, all tears to cease.
A grand reunion with those gone before,
We'll know and be known as we enter the door;
Forever rejoicing, all fears relieved,
A crown of righteousness to be received.
Then at His feet our crown we'll cast
As we bow before Him... Home at last.
No, we do not know what lies ahead...
Only what our Lord has said.
Praise His Holy Name!

"I heard a great voice of much people in heaven, saying,
Alleluia; salvation, and glory, and honour,
and power, unto the Lord our God."
(Rev. 19:1)

CONTENTMENT

Some have little and it's plenty,
While others have much and it's not enough.
When the soul is satisfied, a little is a lot,
But abundance is never enough when it's not.
Thanks be to God who satisfies our hungry, seeking souls.

"What is a man profited, if he gain
the whole world, and lose his own soul?"
"Godliness with contentment is great gain."
(Matt. 16:26; I Tim. 6:6)

WHAT GREATER LOVE?

On a hill call Mount Calvary,
Our Saviour died to set us free.
What Greater Love could ever be...
Than was shown on that rugged tree?

Thus saith the Lord, "I have loved you
with an everlasting love."
(Jer. 31:3)

Faith Messages II

"He is not here, but is risen."
(Luke 24:6)

Faith II

He is Risen

Eternal Life's Door

Eternal Life

Praise His Holy Name

We'll Never Suffer Loss

The Hope of Glory

God's Word Is

Heavenly Treasures

How Could We Ever Thank
Him Enough

Faith

By Faith

Seek First the Kingdom Of God

Where Treasure Is Found

A Place Within

We Just Can't Praise Him
Enough

Free!

Lift Him Up

The Hand of God

The Way of Salvation

He Delivers

We See Him in Nature

Behold the Lamb

Behold His Birth

A Quiet Place

No Room

Behold the Cross

Behold His Resurrection

In Time of Need

Never a Day Passes

He Hears and Answers

Be Still

In His Service

Patience

Listening to God

Written In Our Hearts

Christmas – Is He There?

One Soul

Miracle of All Miracles

Believing Is Seeing

He Always Understands

The Christian "If"

In His Hands

A Debt of Love

God's Holy Laws

The Greatest Commandment

God's Promises

Preparatory School

The Glory of Creation

Indescribable Blessings

ETERNAL LIFE'S DOOR

Simple Faith unlocks The Door to Eternal Life –
It is the Key.
Amazing Grace opens it...
And sets the captive free.

"For by grace are ye saved through faith;
and that not of yourselves:
it is the gift of God:
Not of works, lest any man should boast."
(Eph. 2:8-9)

ETERNAL LIFE

In a fallen state – apart from God,
Sinful, helpless, and lost;
Enjoying the pleasures for a season,
Never stopping to count the cost;
Wandering in darkness far away
From the Shepherd and the fold –
We sense the drawing power of God,
Deep within the soul.
Convicted, we bow in faith – repenting,
As we heed the Master's call,
And our spirit comes alive in Christ,
When we surrender to Him our all.
God imparts His miraculous gift
Of Eternal Life sublime...
And peace and joy fill our hearts
Until the end of time.
Then transported into His presence,
We dwell with Him on high –
"Eye hath not seen, nor ear heard"
What's prepared beyond the sky...
But the glory of Eternal Life
In that pure and Holy place,
Shall surely be that we see our Lord,
And behold His wonderful face.
For it's "Christ in us the hope of glory"
As from this world we flee...
HE IS OUR ETERNAL LIFE,
And forever with Him we'll be.

"For the wages of sin is death; but the gift of God is eternal life
through Jesus Christ our Lord."
(Rom. 6:23)

PRAISE HIS HOLY NAME

He's Jehovah God – The Great "I Am...
Praise His Holy Name!
The Everlasting Father – Creator of all,
From heaven to earth He came.
The Almighty God – The Lord and Master,
The Ruler of all the earth...
Yet, He's our Saviour – our tender Shepherd,
Our guide from time of birth.
He's the Light of the world – the Prince of Glory,
The Lamb sent from afar;
Our abundant Life – our Peace and Joy,
Our Bright and Morning Star.
He's our Deliverer – Shield and Defender,
Our Shelter till the journey's end;
Our Great Physician – our Comforter,
Our Counselor and dearest Friend.
Yesterday, today and forever,
Our God is always the same.
How could we cease to bow before Him...
And Praise His Holy Name?

"Let everything that hath breath praise the Lord.
Praise ye the Lord."
(Ps. 150:6)

WE'LL NEVER SUFFER LOSS

Wars, rumors of wars, perilous times surround;
Conditions are steadily growing worse –
It's evident as we look around.
How can we face what lies ahead? –
We wonder as we see the plight;
Then we remember what our Lord has said...
The battle's not ours to fight.
For it's not by might, nor by power,
But by His Spirit, we're told.
He gives the victory when we look up,
As we see these things unfold.
We lift our heads, and realize –
Our redemption draweth nigh.
Soon we'll enter that glorious place
Prepared for us on High.
No battle shall overcome us,
For the Victor's on our side,
Protecting, shielding, defending us,
As in Him we abide.
The enemy is a defeated foe,
Conquered at the cross.
No weapon formed against us shall prosper,
And We'll Never Suffer Loss.

"And when these things begin to come to pass, then look up,
and lift up your heads; for your redemption draweth nigh."
(Luke 21:28)

THE HOPE OF GLORY

Heaven and earth shall pass away,
But God's Word abideth still...
The Living Word who came into the world
To accomplish the Father's will.
His death on the cross opened the gate
To our home beyond the sky;
And all who bow shall enter in,
To dwell with Him on High.
Yes, heaven and earth shall pass away,
At the end of this thing called time,
But Christ in us is the Hope of Glory...
And eternal life sublime.

"... Christ in you, the hope of glory."
(Col. 1:27)

GOD'S WORD IS

Light in our world of darkness –
A lamp unto our feet.
Food for our hungry souls,
As honeycomb, it is sweet.
Yet, bitter to some when piercing
The thoughts and intents concealed –
Sharper than a two edged sword,
That hearts may be revealed.
It's the water of life for the thirsty –
A fountain freely flowing;
A fire ablaze within our souls,
Continually warm and glowing.
It's the Living Word that was with the Father
Before the world began –
The One who came from glory above
To redeem fallen man,
Fulfilling the law given to all
Under bondage, struggle and strife,
Enabling us to keep His commandments –
God's Word in us Is LIFE.

"In Him was life;
and the life was the light of men."
(John 1:4)

HEAVENLY TREASURES

Treasures come in many forms –
Money, houses, and land,
Cabins in the mountains,
Condos on the sand,
Fancy cars and clothing,
Diamonds, silver, and gold
No good thing is withheld from those
Within the Shepherd's fold.
But, these material gifts we enjoy
As we travel this earthly sod,
Can be a curse, rather than a blessing,
If we let them become our god.
When we love the gift more than the Giver,
We're treading on dangerous ground,
For those things we valued so highly
Aren't the treasures we thought we'd found –
Our souls are left impoverished,
Hungry and thirsty within,
As we find we've left our first Love
And fallen into sin.
I'd rather have nothing of material worth
As I sit at the Master's feet,
Than to have the wealth of all the world –
And miss Heavenly Treasures so sweet.

"Lay not up for yourselves treasures upon earth, but lay up for
yourselves treasures in heaven, where neither moth nor rust doth
corrupt, and where thieves do not break through nor steal:
For where your treasure is, there will be your heart also."
(Matt. 19-21)

How Could We Ever Thank Him Enough

How could we ever thank Him enough
For everything He's done?
He loved this world so very much
He sacrificed His Son.
Oh... the wonder of it all –
That He could love us so,
Bringing us into His kingdom
His blessings to bestow;
Forgiving, cleansing, making us whole,
Imparting new life within our soul...
How could we ever praise Him enough
For His love and mighty power?
His Greatness abounds – His Spirit surrounds;
He's our Refuge – our High Tower.
The Great Majestic Holy God,
Who sits upon His throne...
Yet, our loving, tender Shepherd –
Such mercy He has shown.
Oh God, we worship at Thy footstool,
And praise Thy Holy Name...
But, How Could We Ever Thank You Enough?
Our efforts seem so lame.

"Enter into His gates with thanksgiving, and into His courts with praise:
be thankful unto Him, and bless His name."
(Ps. 100:4)

FAITH

Faith is the key that unlocks the gate
Where spiritual treasures we glean.
It is "the substance of things hoped for –
The evidence of things not seen."
As we enter the gate through faith,
Our blinded eyes can see...
That substance for which we'd hoped –
The evidence of eternity.
Behold! At last it all unfolds –
Those things which satisfy our souls.
Such wonderful treasures
We now have found;
For through Faith we've entered
A higher ground.

"But without faith it is impossible to please Him:
For he that cometh to God must believe that He is,
and that He is a rewarder of them that diligently seek Him."
(Heb. 11:6)

71

BY FAITH

We're justified by faith – we live by faith,
In God's Holy Word we're told;
Just as our fathers of long ago –
The prophets and saints of old.
By faith Enoch walked so close with God...
He was translated into heaven above.
By faith Noah prepared an ark of safety,
As he warned from a heart of love.
By faith Abraham obeyed and went out
Looking for the promised land,
Sojourning in a strange country,
following God's own hand.
By faith Moses led the Hebrews from bondage,
Crossing the sea on dry ground.
By faith Joshua instructed the people to shout!...
And the walls of Jericho fell down.
Faith as a grain of mustard seed
Can move mountains and part the sea,
And the prayer of faith can heal the sick
And set the captive free...
Yes, justified by faith – we live By Faith –
The Faith of the Son of God,
Looking to Him – The Author and Finisher
As on this earth we trod.

"Looking to Jesus the author and finisher of our faith."
(Heb. 12:2)

SEEK FIRST THE KINGDOM OF GOD

We're told to seek first the kingdom of God
And His righteousness,
And all our daily needs will be met
As we surrender and confess.
When we consider the birds of the air
And the lilies of the field,
We know our Father will take care of us
As we look to Him and yield.
So, may we take no anxious thought
For our food and clothing each day,
But always Seek First The Kingdom Of God
And His Holy Righteous Way.

"Seek ye first the kingdom of God,
and His righteousness:
And all these things shall be added unto you."
(Matt. 6:33)

WHERE TREASURE IS FOUND

We could search this world over
And still never find
Those things that give joy
And a satisfied mind;
For the world does not hold
These treasures we seek,
Though its pleasures allure
And of happiness speak;
True joy and satisfaction
Can only be found
As we seek our treasure...
On Higher Ground.

"For He satisfieth the longing soul,
and filleth the hungry soul with goodness."
(Ps. 107:9)

A PLACE WITHIN

There's a deep place within the soul
Where nothing or no one can go.
It is without form and void –
Not a sign of life to show.
Darkness is upon the face of the deep,
Where empty desolation abounds.
Then God says "let there be light" –
And suddenly His Spirit surrounds.
In mercy and love He responds
To the desperate repentant cry...
And now a river freely flows
That never shall run dry.
Hallelujah... There's a new man created
In Christ our living King.
And the angels in heaven rejoice
As they gleefully worship and sing;
For a new name is written down in glory
That no one can erase,
And abundant life now fills the void
By God's amazing grace.
Praise God who is on His Holy throne;
He's a Lord that we can know –
Praise Him for A Place Within
Where only He can go.

"There is joy in the presence of the angels of God
over one sinner that repenteth."
(Luke 15:10)

75

WE JUST CAN'T PRAISE HIM ENOUGH

For our family, friends, and good health,
Days of prosperity and wealth;
For sustaining us in the hard times we face
By His marvelous amazing Grace;
For carrying us through our darkest hour,
As we rest in Him – His strength and power;
For the peace and joy that He provides –
As His Holy Spirit within abides...

WE JUST CAN'T PRAISE HIM ENOUGH!!

For His comfort in times of sorrow,
Giving us hope for a new tomorrow;
For being a friend closer than a brother –
One who loves us like no other;
For supplying all our daily need,
As we look to Him – His word to heed;
For cleansing us and making us His –
But Most of all for Who He Is...

WE JUST CAN'T PRAISE HIM ENOUGH!!

He's The Mighty God – The Alpha and Omega,
The Creator of all the earth,
The Great Shepherd – The Promised Messiah
Who came to give new birth.
He's The Father, The Son and Holy Spirit
Who reveals to us His ways;
The One and only God of the universe –
And He's worthy of ALL OUR PRAISE...

WE JUST CAN'T PRAISE HIM ENOUGH!!

"Great is the Lord, and greatly to be praised."
"Praise Him for His mighty acts:
praise Him according to His excellent greatness."
"Let every thing that hath breath praise the Lord,
Praise ye the Lord."
(Ps. 48:1, 150:2, 6)

76

FREE!

Hallelujah!... We Are Free!!
Free from a heart bound by captivity;
Free from eyes that cannot see;
Free from ears that cannot hear;
Free from a world of darkness and fear;
Free from a life of sin and its toll;
Free from Satan's power and control;
Free from those heavy chains that bind;
Free in our spirit, soul, and mind...

Hallelujah!... We Are Free!!

Free by God's wondrous-amazing grace;
Free by His Son who died in our place;
Free by the precious blood that He shed;
Free by the resurrection from the dead;
Free by His pardon from all our sin;
Free by His cleansing power within;
Free by our Creator's omnipotent hand;
Free as we bow and are born again...

Hallelujah!... We Are Free!!

Free to know peace and true happiness;
Free to enjoy a life that is blessed;
Free to love and forgive our brother;
Free to serve God and one another;
Free to live righteous, holy lives;
Free to follow Christ as He guides;
Free to worship and praise His Name;
Thank God we're FREE from all our shame...

Hallelujah!... We Are Free!!

"Stand fast therefore in the liberty wherewith Christ hath made us
free, and be not entangled again with the yoke of bondage."
(Gal. 5:1)

LIFT HIM UP

Souls are in darkness – searching and lost,
Destroyed and wrecked by sin,
In need of a miracle to make them whole,
In need of God's touch within.
Lift up the Lord – The Christ of God,
For all the world to see...
Whosoever looks to Him for salvation
Shall live eternally.

"As Moses lifted up the serpent in the wilderness,
even so must the Son of man be lifted up."
(John 3:14)

THE HAND OF GOD

It was God's mighty omnipotent Hand
That wrote the ten commandments of law;
And today as we see His Hand at work –
We marvel and stand in awe!
It is the Hand of God that makes us,
The Hand of God that saves us,
The Hand of God that keeps us,
And the Hand of God that leads us.
It is the Hand of God that corrects us,
The Hand of God that protects us,
The Hand of God that heals us,
And the Hand of God that seals us.
It is the Hand of God that justifies,
The Hand of God that purifies,
The Hand of God that sanctifies,
And the Hand of God that glorifies.
It was God's mighty omnipotent Hand
That resurrected Christ our King;
And that same Hand raises us to new life,
Holding us securely under His wing.

It is The Hand of God!

By His Hand, our names are written
In the Lamb's book of life...

"If I take the wings of the morning, and dwell in the uttermost
parts of the sea; Even there thy right hand shall hold me."
(Ps. 139:9-10)

THE WAY OF SALVATION

This world is rocking and reeling with sin.
Sometimes it's hard to trust even a friend.
We've come so far in so many ways;
Yet, sin is the same as in Noah's days.
Technology has really advanced over time;
And we've seen the stock market soar and climb.
Man has such a magnificent, brilliant brain;
But it seems his efforts have all been in vain.
Though we've accomplished much in the world today,
Immorality abounds in the same old way.
We sacrifice our souls for mere temporal things,
And then suffer the consequences it brings.
Where is the profit if we can't trust our neighbor?
And where are the fruits of all our labor?
There's certainly nothing wrong with man's mind,
But his heart and soul are in a terrible bind –
Needing to be freed from the state of sin;
Needing the presence of the Holy Spirit within.
Father, grant true repentance across our land,
And may we, Your people, do all we can.
Help us to repent and turn from our wicked ways,
Glorifying Your Name and giving You praise.
Only then will You begin to heal our nation,
As we proclaim Christ – The Way of Salvation.

"If my people, which are called by my name, shall humble
themselves, and pray, and seek my face, and turn from
their wicked ways; Then will I hear from heaven, and will
forgive their sin, and will heal their land."
(II Ch. 7:14)

HE DELIVERS

God saw the affliction of His people in Egypt,
And heard their desperate cry...
Such love and mercy He's shown through the ages,
When souls to Him draw nigh.
He delivered the Hebrews from oppression and bondage,
Leading every step of the way;
Bringing them to the land of promise,
And a bright, new, glorious day!
That land still flows with milk and honey,
And God still answers the desperate cry...
As in days of old, He still delivers,
When souls to Him draw nigh.

"Seek ye the Lord while he may be found,
call upon him while he is near."
(Is. 55:6)

WE SEE HIM IN NATURE

In the whole realm of nature –
In the sea and on the land,
We see the splendor and glory of God,
And His mighty – omnipotent hand.
The mountains proclaim His majesty;
The valleys His loving care;
And as we look toward heaven above,
We surely see Him there.
The light of the moon and stars
Proclaim His glory and grace,
Lifting our hearts in praise to Him
Who put them in their place.
Oh God, we see You in a garden,
And a tiny little seed;
We see You in a flower,
And a kind and thoughtful deed.
Oh, how we worship and adore You –
Our hearts rejoice and sing;
For we see You everywhere –
And in every single thing.

"The heavens declare the glory of God;
and the firmament sheweth his handywork."
(Ps. 19:1)

BEHOLD THE LAMB

"Behold The Lamb of God, which taketh away the sin..."
Giving peace and joy, cleansing the heart within.
Nothing disturbs Satan and his vast domain
More than this message being proclaimed.
The blood sacrifice of Christ our King
Sets men free... let the message ring.
Satan and his demons have no more control,
As God brings lost sinners into His fold;
Rescuing souls from darkness grim –
Giving new life to abide in Him –
No longer captive behind Satan's door...
Nothing... No Nothing
Shakes hell's gates more.

"Behold the Lamb of God,
which taketh away the sin of the world."
(John 1:29)

BEHOLD HIS BIRTH

"For unto us a child is born,
Unto us a Son is given" –
Leaving His home, He came to earth
From His Father's throne in heaven.
His birth-the fulfillment of prophecy,
Awaited since time began.
The promised Messiah – The sacrificial Lamb –
The Saviour of fallen man.
Born of a virgin in an humble stable –
No room for Him in the Inn,
The only begotten Son of God
Came to take away our sin.
His birth-announced by the Angel of the Lord
To the Shepherds out in the field,
As the Glory of God shone round about –
The good news was revealed:
"For unto you is born this day in the city of David
A Saviour, which is Christ the Lord."
Then suddenly there was a multitude of the heavenly host
Praising God again and again...
Saying "Glory to God in the highest,
And on earth peace, good will toward men."
Behold what a glorious proclamation
Of our Lord and Saviour's birth;
A babe in a manger in Bethlehem –
Our King come down to earth.
Lo, there was a star in the east
Leading the wise men to where He lay...
They saw Him – and fell down and worshipped –
Hallelujah!! What a Glorious Day!!

Glory to God!!

"... and thou shalt call his name JESUS:
for he shall save his people from their sins."
(Matt. 1:21)

84

A QUIET PLACE

He bypassed the noise of the busy city,
Choosing the quiet serenity of a field,
Where watchful shepherds, tending their flock,
Had prayerful hearts – ready to yield.
It was there, a quiet place, God sent His angel
With the most important message on earth...
The proclamation of the Messiah's coming-
The Lord and Saviour's birth.
God still chooses a quiet place
To speak His message to men.
He seeks prayerful hearts – ready to yield,
Just as He did back then.
Many are too busy to listen
To the message He would speak,
And the Holy Spirit passes on by –
A quiet place to seek.
Oh, God, we pray You'd not pass us by,
But may we always have within –
A Quiet Place prepared to receive
The message You would send.

"A meek and quiet spirit... is in
the sight of God of great price."
(I Pet. 3:4)

85

NO ROOM

He was born in an humble stable –
No room for Him in the Inn.
The same story seems to prevail today –
No room in this world of sin.
There's room for entertainment and pleasure,
Selfish pursuits and material treasure;
Plenty of room for whatever we desire –
Those Ambitious goals for which we aspire;
But, are we making the same mistake again?
Is there no room for Jesus in the lives of men?
No room for Him in our hearts here?
Will there be room for us in heaven there?
Oh, Father, clean out the clutter within.
May we, your people, be free of sin –
A place prepared without the dust...
More room for You, and less of us.

"He must increase, but I must decrease."
(John 3:30)

BEHOLD THE CROSS

Behold the cross where our Saviour died,
Where His precious blood was shed...
Behold His suffering and agony –
The thorns upon His head.
Behold His nail pierced hands –
The spikes driven in His feet.
See the blood flow from His side –
Into the mercy seat.
Hear the pain in His voice that cried,
"Father forgive them;
For they know not what they do."
Then the final cry, "It is finished." –
The penalty paid, for me and you.
Oh, what a sacrifice made for man!
Oh, such love within God's plan!

Behold The Cross

"Christ died for the ungodly."
"... the precious blood of Christ,
as a lamb without blemish or spot."
(Rom. 5:6; I Pet. 1:19)

BEHOLD HIS RESURRECTION

"Why come to this place seeking the living among the dead?
He is not here... He is Risen!" – The heavenly messengers said.
Hallelujah... He's Alive!... Alive forevermore!
He arose, just as He said He would, and opened glory's door.
Without His resurrection... There'd be no salvation, no justification,
There'd be no purification, no sanctification.
Without His resurrection... There'd be no redemption story;
There'd be no Hope of Glory.
Praise God... our King is alive and well –
He's conquered all... sin, death, and hell.
Take the message everywhere... Go and tell:
Resurrected...He's The WAY for all who relent,
Believing in Him, as they bow and repent;
Resurrected... He's The TRUTH for all who seek –
Having ears to hear what God would speak;
Resurrected... He's The LIFE for the spiritually dead –
Quickened and cleansed by the blood He shed.
Praise the Name of JESUS... Praise Him forevermore –
Our Saviour is alive today,
And He's Heaven's only door.

Hallelujah... He's Alive!

Jesus said, "I am the way, the truth, and the life:
no man cometh unto the Father, but by me."
(John 14:6)

In Time of Need

Whatever trials may come –
However dark the hour,
At the Throne of grace we find...
Mercy, strength and power.
God will not forsake His people,
In His precious Word we read...
His grace is all sufficient,
And comes just In Time of Need.

"Let us therefore come boldly unto the throne of grace,
that we may obtain mercy, and find grace
to help in time of need."
(Heb. 4:16)

NEVER A DAY PASSES

Never a day passes –
Never a moment goes by,
That we don't need our Saviour
And His mercies from on High.
Some days are dark and cloudy,
And we could use a friend –
"What a Friend We Have in Jesus" –
He is faithful to the end.
The times we fail our Master,
And begin to go astray,
"The Way of the Cross Leads Home,"
And helps us find our way.
When there's trouble all around,
And we become distressed,
"Tis so Sweet to Trust in Jesus" –
Just to lean upon His breast.
When trials and hardships come,
And we feel our hearts would break,
"Take it to The Lord in Prayer,"
Our souls He'll not forsake.
And when we need an extra portion
Of His tender loving care,
"Jesus Spreads His Banner O'er Us,"
And keeps us sheltered there.
Then when all is going well,
And the day is sunny and bright,
May we "Yield Not to Temptation,"
But rejoice in Christ, our Light.
Never a day passes –
Never a moment goes by
That we don't need our Saviour,
And His mercies from on High.

"Great are Thy tender mercies, O Lord."
(Ps. 119:156)

HE HEARS AND ANSWERS

There are times so difficult and hard to bear,
We feel we just can't cope;
But, when we take it to our Lord in prayer
We find there's always hope.
He's touched with each infirmity –
His Holy Spirit's nigh.
He knows just what we're going through,
And always hears our cry.
Though circumstances may not change
The way we think they should,
He Answers each and every prayer
For His glory and our good.
Thank You, Father, that we can rely
On your tender loving care,
And that you always Hear and Answer
Every single prayer.

"He shall call upon me, and I will answer him."
(Ps. 91:15)

BE STILL

So many things to do
In this busy world today;
We're constantly on the move
As we work and as we play.
Oh, how we need to come aside
From all the activity,
And just be still before our Maker
As we think on eternity.
Though we may walk close with Him
In fellowship each day,
It's important to have that special time
To bow our hearts and pray.
Just to pause and give Him thanks
For all the love He's shown,
As we humbly kneel and worship
Before His Holy Throne.
In the quietness of our spirit
He'll speak His perfect will,
As we learn to listen with our hearts,
And just be very still.

"Be still and know that I am God."
(Ps. 46:10)

IN HIS SERVICE

As we work in the kingdom of God –
Planting and sowing the seed,
Giving our lives in service
To help a friend in need,
Our hearts can become discouraged,
When, in spite of all we've done,
The circumstances remain unchanged –
The victory not yet won.
But, then a still small voice within
Speaks this message clear and bold:
"Keep your eyes on Me, my child,
As you work within the fold,
And I will give you perfect peace
Within your heart and soul."
Father, thank You that we can rejoice,
Knowing You are faithful and true,
And as we labor in Thy service,
May we leave the results with You.

"Thou wilt keep him in perfect peace,
whose mind is stayed on Thee."
(Is. 26:3)

PATIENCE

Oh, how we need patience
In our busy world today;
We have so many things to do
There's hardly time to pray.
Our calendars are so filled
That when we need to help a friend,
We find our patience running short –
Our schedules just won't bend.
Father, help us to be flexible,
And always follow Your lead,
As we help our friends
In their time of need.
We pray we'd have tender hearts
That truly understand,
Willing to go the extra mile
For our fellowman.
May our priorities always be
What You'd have them to be –
The needs of others first –
The things of eternity.
Give us empathy, and patience
That comes only from You,
And help us to be Christ-like
In everything we do.

"Be patient toward all men."
(I Thes. 5:14)

94

LISTENING TO GOD

Sometimes we talk too much
To hear what God would say.
Other times we're preoccupied
With activities of the day.
Oh, how we need to just be quiet,
And listen with our hearts
To what the Holy Spirit speaks –
The truth that He imparts.
He speaks to us through nature,
Where we see His mighty hand.
He speaks through our circumstances,
And through our fellowman.
Through a still small voice within,
We hear what He would say,
As we look to Him for guidance,
Along our pilgrim way.
But, we need to always examine
That which we have heard,
Making sure it's in accordance
With His Holy Written Word –
For God never directs contrary
To what is written there.
The law He gave so long ago
Still applies to all everywhere.
Father, thank You that as we listen,
Your Spirit leads us right,
Impressing the message on our Hearts
That's written in black and white.

"This book of the law shall not depart out of thy mouth;
but thou shalt meditate therein day and night,
that thou mayest observe to do according to all
that is written therein: for then thou shalt make
thy way prosperous, and then shalt thou have good success."
(Josh. 1:8)

WRITTEN IN OUR HEARTS

God made a new covenant
For all who would come,
In faith believing
In His only Son.
The sacrifice made
On Mount Calvary,
Ushered in the new covenant
That sets men free...
Free from the old –
It's bondage and fear;
Free to know God,
And to feel Him near.
He forgives and removes sin,
Remembering it no more,
And becomes our loving Father
As never before.
Praise God for the new covenant,
And the life He imparts,
As His Holy Law
Is Written In Our Hearts.

"After those days, saith the Lord, I will put my law
in their inward parts, and write it in their hearts,
and will be their God, and they shall be my people."
(Jer. 31:32)

CHRISTMAS – IS HE THERE?

Christmas trees all trimmed with care;
Santa and his helpers everywhere;
Stores so crowded – they overflow;
Presents, goodies, lights all aglow;
Festivities of the holidays – such fun to enjoy;
Stockings filled for each girl and boy...
But, can we find the Saviour anywhere?
Do we see the incomparable Christ – Is He there?
Among all the tinsel, is the sacred in our midst?
Are hearts really filled with heavenly bliss?
As the cash registers ring without cease,
Do faces reflect true joy and peace?
Sometimes our hearts cry out, "Deliver us from this season" –
Then we come aside, and focus on Him – who is the reason.
Such a Holy event – His coming to earth,
God's only begotten Son – a virgin birth.
Lord, help us to truly celebrate,
As we slow down, and quietly meditate.
Guard our hearts through all the fanfare...
Help us to worship, and know You are there.

"Follow peace with all men and holiness,
without which no man shall see the Lord."
(Heb. 12:14)

ONE SOUL

It was for each one – individually,
Our Lord and Saviour came.
The hairs of our head numbered,
He knew us by name;
And Had there been just one
Dwelling on this earth –
He still would have come
To give that one new birth.
The only begotten Son of God-
The holy, perfect Seed,
Would still have sacrificed His life
For One Soul to be freed...
Such Love!

"The very hairs of your head
are all numbered."
(Matt. 10:30)

MIRACLE OF ALL MIRACLES

Natural eyes opened – the spiritual to behold.
Stony hearts softened – once hard and cold.
Deaf ears unstopped – hear the joyful sound.
Silent voices speak – God's message all around.
Feeble knees bow – finding strength for the day.
Restless feet turn – to walk the narrow way.
Selfish hands grasping – now reach out to give.
Sinful souls, spiritually dead – given new life to live.
Praise God for the Miracle of all Miracles
Wrought by His mighty power,
Transforming lives even this hour.

"A new heart also will I give you,
and a new spirit will I put within you."
(Eze. 36:26)

BELIEVING IS SEEING

In the natural world – "Seeing is believing",
But in God's kingdom – "Believing is seeing".
When through faith we believe in God's only Son,
By grace we receive, and the victory's won.
Christ is the light, and the kingdom's door –
Through which we enter to dwell evermore.
In Him there's no darkness – we now can see...
Our spiritual eyes opened – our souls set free.
We see those things from up above –
God's mighty power and wondrous love.
We see Him as our dearest friend,
And feel His presence deep within.
We see Him as our defender and shield,
As we rest in Him – our all to yield.
We see Him as our rock and stay –
The One who keeps us day by day.
We see Him as our joy and peace –
A fountain flowing without cease.
We see a portion of His glory bright,
No longer in darkness – we see the light.
Thank You, Father, for the vision You give,
As we believe on Christ – and in Him live.

"He that seeth me, seeth him that sent me.
I am come a light into the world, that whosoever believeth on me
should not abide in darkness."
(John 12:45-46)

HE ALWAYS UNDERSTANDS

When our best seems not enough,
And somehow we've missed the mark –
When misunderstood by others,
And the day is dreary and dark –
Our precious Lord lights our way
As He holds us in His hands,
Encouraging our weary souls –
He always understands.
His grace is all sufficient
When we find our spirits low;
And though our flesh is very weak,
Divine strength we can know.
As we sense His tender loving care,
Undergirding – lifting us up,
Giving assurance of His faithfulness,
Filling our empty cup,
Our spirits are revived –
Rejoicing floods our souls –
Vibrant vessels once again
Ready to serve within the fold.
Christ is the Light when all is dark,
And we've missed our goals and plans.
He's the stabilizing force beneath our wings,
And He Always Understands.

"Thou knowest my downsitting and my uprising,
Thou understandest my thought afar off."
(Ps. 139:2)

THE CHRISTIAN "IF"

If you can keep your moral standards high
When all about are yielding to the tempter's charms;
If you can trust God, and love Him supremely,
Resting completely in your Saviour's arms;
If you can love your neighbor as yourself,
Going the second mile in time of need,
Then move on as though you'd done nothing,
And never breath a word about your deed:

If you can pray and not make prayers a substitute
For action when there's a call for such;
If you can witness to those about you
With the love and humility of the Master's touch;
If you can meet with rejection and hatred
As did our Lord while walking on this earth,
And selflessly persevere in the battle
For souls to have new spiritual birth:

If you can go through trials and hardships
And never murmur or complain,
Enabled to look up and rejoice
Regardless of the suffering or pain;
If you can trust, with full assurance
Of a divine purpose for the test,
Knowing all is working for God's glory,
As well as for your best:

If you have a hunger for righteousness
In this world of immorality and sin;
If you detest the thought of displeasing God,
And your heart's desire is purity within;
If you thirst for the truth of the Holy Scriptures –
God's written word to fallen men,
Yours is the kingdom of God and all that's in it,
And – what's more – you have eternal life, my friend!

"... and of His kingdom there shall be no end."
(Luke 1:33)

IN HIS HANDS

Tragedy strikes so suddenly
Changing all our plans;
More than ever we realize
Our lives are in His hands:
Hands – so strong and mighty
Protect us day by day,
Guarding our hearts and minds
When troubles come our way.
Hands – so warm and loving,
Strengthen and give release,
In the midst of the raging battle
There's a deep settled peace.
Hands – so comforting and caring
Undergird in our darkest hour,
Carrying us through rough waters
As we rest in sovereign power.
Father, thank You for holding us securely
In Your strong omnipotent Hands;
Help us to submit completely
To Your perfect will and plans.

"The Lord is good, a strong hold in the day of trouble."
(Nahum 1:7)

A DEBT OF LOVE

Not willing any should perish,
God's love extends to all...
The sacrificial death on Calvary –
Redemption from the fall.
A love deeper than the ocean,
Reaching far and wide –
Receptive hearts are blessed,
As in Him they abide.
Such a debt of love we owe
For our Saviour's life laid down,
And as we onward go,
May we evermore be found
Loving others as He loved us –
Giving our lives for our friends;
Serving as our Saviour leads,
Until our journey ends.

"Love one another, as I have loved you.
Greater love hath no man than this,
that a man lay down his life for his friends."
(John 15:12-13)

GOD'S HOLY LAWS

The ten commandments given by God,
On that mountain so long ago,
Are His holy laws for all mankind,
That His righteous way we'd know.
Plainly written in His Word,
Too clear to misunderstand,
Bringing conviction to our hearts
In keeping with His plan.
In light of His righteousness and holiness,
We bow on bended knee,
Repenting and confessing our sin –
As the Saviour sets us free...
By His shed blood we're liberated
From the bondage of guilt and sin,
And now the commandments we could not keep
Are indelibly written within.
Christ came not to make void the law,
But that it would be fulfilled –
As we walk in fellowship with Him –
His Spirit in us revealed.
Father, may we always keep your holy laws,
Never to go astray.
Thank You for enabling grace
As we abide in You each day.

"I delight to do thy will, O my God: yea, thy law is within my heart."
(Ps. 40:8)

THE GREATEST COMMANDMENT

Of all the commandments given,
The greatest one is love.
The scriptures teach so clearly –
"First love God above."
We're to love Him with all our heart,
And with all our mind and soul;
Love Him above all else,
In our youth, and when we're old.
This is the most important law,
As taught by Christ Himself;
And the second is like unto it –
"Love your neighbor as yourself."
On these two commandments
Hang all laws – falling into place,
As we bear the fruit of God's love...
Reaching out to the human race.

"Thou shalt love the Lord thy God with all thy heart,
and with all thy soul, and with all thy mind.
This is the first and great commandment.
And the second is like unto it,
thou shalt love thy neighbour as thyself."
(Matt. 22:37-39)

GOD'S PROMISES

God never promised there'd be no trouble –
No hardship for you and me,
But He promised to always be with us
Whatever the trial may be.
He never promised sunshine only
Freedom from storms and rain,
But He promised the difficult times
Would work for our spiritual gain.
He promised to be our Shelter,
And cover us with His hand;
The Rock upon which our feet are planted –
Stability in a weary land.
He promised to be our Light in darkness,
And guide our steps each day;
Our tender loving Comforter
When heartaches come our way.
He promised to be our Teacher,
Revealing His will and plan,
Teaching us to trust Him
When we fail to understand.
The lessons we learn through suffering
Qualify us for the Highest Degree,
As we become more like Jesus –
Prepared for eternity.

"For I reckon that the sufferings of this present time
are not worthy to be compared with the glory
which shall be revealed in us."
(Rom. 8:18)

PREPARATORY SCHOOL

Life is a preparatory school:
The Teacher – The Holy Spirit
The Textbook – The Bible
The Assistant – The preacher
The Students – All mankind
The Lessons – The Truth
For spirit, soul and mind
Graduation Day – Departure –
A time of celebration
Award – The Highest Degree –
Eternal Life – Glorification!
Many who attend turn a deaf ear
To what the Teacher would say,
And leave the school unprepared
For Graduation Day.
Father, prepare our hearts to meet You;
May we pass each and every test,
Graduating into Glory
To receive Your very best.

"When he, the Spirit of truth, is come,
he will guide you into all truth."
(John 16:13)

THE GLORY OF CREATION

There's a glory of the sun and moon,
And of every twinkling star,
Declaring the wondrous love of God
From His mighty throne afar.
Each beam brightly flickering forth
Proclaims His glory and grace,
Reaching deep within the soul
Lighting the darkest place.
The glorious beauty of a sunrise
Engulfs the heart in rapture,
And the radiant glow of a sunset...
No artist's brush can capture.
Whenever we look toward heaven,
The magnificent sea, or land,
We stand in awe of majestic splendor
Created by God's own hand.
Each and every creature included –
Beautiful by His design,
Having a glory all their own...
No poet can define.
Praise God for The Glory of Creation –
The bodies that are terrestrial,
But most of all for the Glory of Christ,
And new creatures in Him celestial.

"There are celestial bodies, and bodies terrestrial: but the glory
of the celestial is one, and the glory of the terrestrial is another."
(I Cor. 15:40)

INDESCRIBABLE BLESSINGS

No poet's pen could e'er describe
The glories of our King;
Nor human tongue proclaim the joys
That cause our hearts to sing.
No words in any language
Could portray His Majesty;
Nor explain the glow within the being
Of a sinful soul set free.
No form of communication,
In modern times or old,
Could e'er relate His perfect peace
Imparted to the soul.
Beyond all mortal expression,
Abundant blessings flow,
Reaching hearts at the foot of the cross
With a portion of heaven to know.
Father, thank You for the wondrous glories
Of Christ our Lord and King,
And for the Indescribable Blessings
Knowing Him doth bring.

"Ye rejoice with joy unspeakable and full of glory."
(I Pet. 1:8)

Faith Messages III

"Great is the Lord, and greatly to be praised
in the city of our God, in the mountain on his holiness."
(Psalms 48:1)

Faith III

How Great Thou Art

GREATER THAN ALL

God is greater than All:
All the trials we face each day,
All temptations that come our way,
All insecurities and fears,
All heartaches and tears,
All suffering and pain,
All loss and All gain.
Praise God!
He's Greater Than All.

"Greater is He that is in you,
than he that is in the world."
(I John 4:4)

ASK

God's listening ear is always open
To our humble plea,
And His loving hand is always ready
To lead when we can't see.
His Holy Spirit guides
As we look above and pray,
And His precious Word lights the paths
We travel every day.
His amazing grace provides,
No matter what the task,
When in faith we come to Him,
And just very simply... Ask.

"Ye have not, because ye ask not."
"All things whatsoever ye ask
in prayer, believing, ye shall receive."
(Jas. 4:2; Matt. 21:22)

OUR FAITHFUL SHEPHERD

There are some dry, barren lands we must cross
As God's beloved sheep;
There are dark valleys, difficult mountains,
Some waters rough and deep.
There are enemies to encounter,
Battles to be fought,
Storms to endure,
Lessons to be taught.
Through it all, our Shepherd is faithful,
As our eyes are fixed on Him:
He's the water of life in a dry thirsty land,
The light in the valley dim;
He undergirds as we climb steep mountains,
And carries us through waters deep;
He protects us from the angry wolves
Who seek to harm His sheep;
He fights our battles for us,
And shelters us in the storm,
Teaching us to trust Him
As He keeps us safe and warm.
Praise the Name of Jesus –
The Shepherd of our soul;
We're the people of His pasture –
And He's faithful to His fold.

"The Lord is my shepherd; I shall not want."
"For he is our God; and we are the people of
his pasture, and the sheep of his hand."
(Ps. 23:1; Ps. 95:7)

THE MASTER GARDENER

The Master Gardener finds fertile soil –
A broken, contrite heart,
And plants the seed of faith –
A fruit garden to impart.
Showers from the water of life
Fall upon the ground,
And the warm light of His glory
Shines forth all around.
As the Master cultivates
With His own skillful hand,
Much wonderful fruit is produced –
The sweetest known to man;
A fruit that nourishes the heart,
Once perishing and cold,
And satisfies the hunger
Of the earnest seeking soul.
The crop is plenteous,
There's enough to give away
To those within the family,
And others we meet each day.
May we yield to The Master Gardener
And always be ready to share,
As we walk in His Holy Spirit –
Our lives His fruit to bear.

"The fruit of the Spirit is love, joy, peace, longsuffering,
gentleness, goodness, faith, meekness, temperance:
against such there is no law."
"If we live in the Spirit, let us also walk in the Spirit."
(Gal. 5:22-23, 25)

THE MASTER ARTIST

The Master Artist takes His brush,
And with just one stroke of His hand
Paints the most spectacular portraits
Ever seen by man.
The bright glory of a sunrise
Sends our hearts in rapture,
And the colorful brilliance of a sunset
No mortal's brush could capture.
As we see the moon and stars
We stand in awe of such a glow,
And praise The Master Artist
As we view His work from below.
His handiwork is seen all around –
On land, and sky, and sea,
As well as in every form of life
Including you and me.
Each and every one is unique,
Made beautiful by His touch;
An original masterpiece
Of great value – worth so much.
His work is magnificent –
Every piece a glorious site,
For He's The Master Artist…
And Creator of The Light.

"And God said, Let there be light:
and there was light."
(Gen. 1:3)

THE FIVE SPIRITUAL SENSES

Sight
Could e'er there be a more awesome sight
For human eyes to behold,
Than the vision of the crucified Lord
Resurrected to make men whole?
Sound
Could e'er there be a more beautiful sound
To the ears of mortal men,
Than that joyful melody ringing out
Of a heart set free from sin?
Taste
Could e'er there be a more pleasant taste
Than the word of the living God,
As it feeds the hungry hearts of men,
Directing the paths they trod?
Smell
Could e'er there be a sweeter smell
Than the fragrant heavenly Dove,
As He breathes upon His people,
Filling them with His love?
Touch
Could e'er there be a more precious touch
Than that of the Master's hand –
Forgiving, healing, holding us securely
Till we enter the promised land?

Father, thank you that your blessings
Reach the senses of the heart,
Satisfying our deepest longings…
As they touch each and every part.

"Blessed be the God and Father of our Lord Jesus Christ,
who hath blessed us with all spiritual blessings
in heavenly places in Christ."
(Eph. 1:3)

ETERNAL LOVE

Nothing in this world or any other,
Could separate us from God's love –
No principalities or powers below,
Nor even the angels up above.
No things present, or things to come,
In the whole span of time,
Could ever break the precious bond
Of Eternal Love sublime.
No sphere of space we travel
Could take us from His Love,
Though we sink to the depths of the ocean,
Or soar to great heights above.
Life itself – with it's glittering charms,
Holds no attraction at all,
Compared with the love of God
And the sweet Holy Spirit's call.
Even when death comes nigh our dwelling,
Surrounding us with darkness grim,
The Light of God's Love sustains us
As our eyes are focused on Him.
Father, thank You that no creature exists
That can separate us from Thee,
And thank You that Your Love endures
Throughout time and eternity.

"For I am persuaded, that neither death, nor life, nor angels,
nor principalities, nor powers, nor things present, nor things to come,
nor height, nor depth, nor any other creature, shall be able to
separate us from the love of God, which is in Christ Jesus our Lord."
(Rom. 8:38-39)

THE GOODNESS OF GOD

God Gives...
Peace – in the midst of turmoil
Underlying joy – in time of sorrow
Strength – for today's hardships
New vision – for tomorrow
Calmness – in the storms of life
Grace – in time of need
Love – in the midst of hatred
Charity – in place of greed
Cheerfulness - where there's gloom
Faith – when there is doubt
Light – in the midst of darkness
Hope – to those without
Healing – where there's sickness
Comfort – in times of grief
Wisdom – to those who ask
Knowledge – to souls who seek
Guidance – to all who'll follow
Instruction – to ears that hear
Rest – to the heavy laden
Security – in place of fear
Salvation – to the lost and perishing
Forgiveness – where there's sin
Life – to the spiritually dead
Purity – within

How could we cease to be amazed
at The Goodness of God?

"The goodness of God endureth continually."
(Ps. 52:1)

AMAZING LOVE

No other love in all the world
Could ever begin to compare
With the sacrificial love at Calvary,
As Christ paid our sin debt there.
The pain and suffering He endured
Upon that old rugged tree,
Proclaimed so loud and clear –
God's love for you and me.
Each precious drop of blood that fell,
As He hung there in our place,
Shouts echoes through all ages
Of His mercy and His grace.
The most Amazing Love known to man
Expressed upon that mountain –
Now springing up within our hearts –
An ever flowing fountain.
How could we cease to give honor and glory
To our heavenly Father above?
How could we ever cease to praise Him
For such AMAZING LOVE?

"For God so loved the world, that he gave his only
begotten Son, that whosoever believeth in him
should not perish, but have everlasting life."
(John 3:16)

SUFFERING PERSECUTION

Should we ever think it strange
When hated and reviled
By those outside the Shepherd's fold,
Living their lives defiled?
Should we despair when rejected
By those not living right –
Imprisoned in a state of darkness,
Unable to see the Light?
Should we wonder why we're ridiculed,
And often falsely accused,
By the self-righteous religionists
Who all their sin excuse?
Should we be perplexed
When persecuted on every hand
By the enemies of our Lord
Who do not understand?
Christ, Himself, suffered these things
At the hands of men who hate,
And He instructs His people to be glad,
For our reward in heaven is great.
We're to persevere with all the saints,
As we share the redemption story;
It will be worth it all when we get home –
And rejoice with Him in Glory!

"Beloved, think it not strange concerning the fiery trial which is to try you,
as though some strange thing happened unto you: But rejoice,
inasmuch as ye are partakers of Christ's sufferings; that when his glory
shall be revealed, ye may be glad also with exceeding joy."
(I Pet. 4:12-13)

HIS PRESENCE

God is not seen with the physical eye,
Nor heard with the natural ear,
But we sense His Holy Spirit
And feel His presence, oh, so near.
As we read His precious word,
It's then we understand –
We see Him through His only Son
When we are born again.
We see His hand of guidance
As we seek His will and way –
Following the paths of righteousness,
We see Him every day.
We hear Him speak loud and clear
Through that still small voice within,
Correcting us when we go astray –
Keeping our lives from sin.
He whispers sweet peace to our hearts –
Greater than any earthly treasure;
And the joy we have in His presence
Far surpasses worldly pleasure.
Our God is not a harsh, distant Father,
Way off beyond the blue –
He's always right here with us
In everything we do.
And as we humbly walk before Him,
Our hearts yielded in prayer,
The keen awareness of His Presence
Leaves no doubt – our Lord is there!

"In his presence is fullness of joy."
(Ps. 16:11)

SATISFACTION

The hunger and thirst within one's soul,
Can only be quenched as his spirit's made whole.
The emptiness within man's heart, God alone can fill;
And the anxiety and restlessness, only He can still.
No earthly treasure can answer the desperate cry,
Nor can any worldly pleasure ever satisfy;
But a hungry seeking soul kneeling to God in prayer,
Always finds satisfaction and contentment there –
Looking to Jesus, responding to His call,
Confessing sin, surrendering all –
The search is ended, there's sweet release,
The heart overflows with joy and peace.
Father, thank You for filling the void
With blessings from above,
And for satisfying our hunger and thirst
With Your wondrous grace and love.

"For he satisfieth the longing soul,
and filleth the hungry soul with goodness."
(Ps. 107:9)

ANSWERED PRAYER

God drew us to His Son and took our sins away;
Could we ever doubt He hears us when we pray?
He heard as we cried out far from the Shepherd's fold,
And by His grace and power – He made us whole.
Now as His sheep, walking close, sheltered in His care,
How could we ever doubt He hears and answers prayer?
Sometimes the answer is "yes," sometimes "no," or "wait,"
But always in His perfect time – never a moment late;
And if we pray for healing and our thorn is left to bear,
It's never because our Lord doesn't hear or care;
A much greater work is being done, as He strengthens us within
Conforming us to the image of Christ, perhaps to help a friend;
Or He's simply drawing us closer, loving us even more,
Teaching us to trust Him more than ever before.
And when He grants our petition, making the answer clear,
Should we be amazed as we see His hand so near?
Perhaps not, but I never cease to be amazed
At God's goodness, love and care,
As I see His awesome power, revealed in Answered Prayer.

"He shall call upon me, and I will answer him."
(Ps. 91:15)

FERTILE GROUND

Pastors and teachers must prepare
When sowing God's precious seed,
And our hearts must be prepared
With the fertile soil we need;
Lest the seed be snatched away,
Christ having been denied,
The Word never entering the heart –
Life's seed... by the wayside.
And that which falls on stony ground –
Hardened, rocky clay,
Has no root, and soon dries up,
In time withering away.
And when it falls among the thorns
Of worldly cares, riches and lusts,
The Word is choked, making unfruitful
That seed which was sown in us.
But, when the soil is soft and fertile,
The seed of life can grow,
And as it takes root, producing fruit,
The love of Christ will show.
Oh, God, we ask you'd plow our soil,
Breaking up the clots that are found,
That the seeds sown in Your temple
Would fall on Fertile Ground.

"And these are they which are sown on good ground;
such as hear the word, and receive it, and bring forth fruit."
(Mark 4:20)

SIN'S DANGER

Never fear trials and hardships,
Or heavy burdens given to bear,
For strength comes in time of need,
When sheltered in God' s care.
But fear sin... it is a deadly poison,
And like a venomous snake,
It will coil itself around us,
Our very lives to take.
Praise God for the old rugged cross,
And the victory over sin;
As we submit our all to Christ,
He keeps us pure within.
Lord, thank You for being our refuge
From sin's dangerous snare;
We pray we'd never stray away
From Your protective care.

"Submit yourselves unto God,
Resist the devil, and he will flee from you."
(James 4:7)

HOLY GROUND

Through Christ, our Lord and Master,
We've a portion of heaven's ground,
Where we sense the Holy Spirit's
Sweet presence all around.
Do our hearts not burn within,
As He teaches us His way?
Are we not in awe of His majesty,
As we see His hand each day?
In our Heavenly Father's presence,
A deep peace is found,
As we realize we're standing
On Holy Ground!

"Did not our hearts burn within us,
while he talked with us by the way,
and while he opened to us the scriptures?"
(Luke 24:32)

FAR BETTER

Far better to worship at God's footstool
Surrendering all earthly gain,
Than to live luxuriously in Satan's palace
Sin and self to reign.

Far better to walk in rough, dark waters
With God's presence all around,
Than to sail smoothly in the bright sunlight
Away from holy ground.

Far better to have no place to lay our head
Following Christ each day,
Than to sleep in the finest mansion
Going Satan's way.

Far better to be a worn, useful vessel,
Filled and serving the King,
Than a beautiful empty vase on the shelf
Never doing anything.

Far better to be our Master's servant
Obeying His every command,
Than to be a great and mighty ruler
Bound by Satan's hand.

Lord, we'd rather have nothing
And live for Thee,
Than to have the whole world
And not be free.

Far Better!

"I had rather be a doorkeeper in the house of my God,
than to dwell in the tents of wickedness."
(Ps. 84:10)

THE GOSPEL LIGHT

To take the Son of God from religion,
Is to take the sun right out of the sky.
It is to remove all joy and victory –
All blessings from on high.
It is to take away the moon and stars,
Leaving only the darkest night –
No glorious ray lighting our path,
No vision, no hope, no sight.
If Christ be not the heart of the gospel,
Then there's no foundation or core.
Laws and doctrines cannot save us –
We're all lost forevermore.
But, Praise God, He Is The Gospel –
Let us lift His Name on high...
That souls who dwell in darkness
Would see the Light and draw nigh.

"For other foundation can no man lay
than that is laid, which is Jesus Christ."
(I Cor. 3:11)

MIDDLE GROUND

God forbid we stand on middle ground –
Neither cold nor hot;
Let us believe Christ with all our heart,
Or either believe Him not.
Believe the precious Word of God,
Every bit and part,
Or else reject it all,
And from the Truth depart.
Lukewarm Christians do more harm
In the work of eternity,
Than those who've never believed
The Truth that sets men free.
We cannot serve two masters,
We'll hate one and love the other;
Therefore, let us whole heartedly serve God,
And, with fervent hearts, our brother.
Father, deliver us from Middle Ground –
The state of indifference and apathy.
Give us convictions strong and bold,
And hearts on fire for Thee.

"I would thou wert cold or hot."
"Ye cannot serve God and mammon."
(Rev. 3:15; Matt. 6:24)

A RAINY DAY

At times when it rains outside,
We let it rain within,
Until we look above and see...
God knows just what to send.
Without rain, no gardens would grow;
There'd be no beauty of Spring;
No fruit would be in the vineyard;
No bountiful crop to bring.
Without life's difficulties and hardships,
Our hearts would never know
The nurturing tender care of the Father,
And our souls would never grow.
There'd be no fruit in our lives to share
With our sister and our brother;
No genuine empathy or compassion
Would be felt for one another.
Father, help us to always give thanks
For the trials that come our way,
Knowing You're growing spiritual fruit
When we face A Rainy Day.

"And the rain descended, and the floods came,
and the winds blew, and beat upon that house;
and it fell not: for it was founded upon a rock."
(Matt. 7:25)

STRENGTH AND GRACE

Beneath our heaviest burden,
There's a strength beyond compare –
An underlying, mighty power,
Lifting the load we cannot bear.
Beneath a thorn in the flesh
That may never go away,
Is a grace that's all sufficient
To carry us through the day.
God's omnipotent hand undergirds,
As we yield within His fold,
Surrendering all to the Shepherd –
Our will under His control.
Whatever the trial or tribulation,
His Spirit is always there,
Drawing us closer to Himself,
Revealing His loving care.
Father, thank You for Strength and Grace
Provided for Your sheep.
May we completely submit to You
Our hearts and souls to keep.

"And he said unto me, My grace is sufficient for thee:
for my strength is made perfect in weakness."
(II Cor. 12:9)

THE TURBULENT SEA

The worst trials we face as Christians,
The biggest, roughest waves,
Just move us closer to our goal
As the angry storm raves.
Those things we count our greatest loss
Can become our greatest gain;
Even sickness becomes our health
As we're strengthened through the pain.
Though we never desire a trial,
Nor welcome a spiritual test,
We know each one, though grievous at first,
Is working for our best.
And underneath the turbulent sea
Of heartache, trouble, and tears,
Our anchor holds securely
Relieving all our fears.
Then when the waters have calmed,
And the boisterous winds cease,
There is, oh, such an awareness
Of inner joy and peace.
Father, thank you for The Turbulent Sea
That brings us closer to You.
We pray we'd use the lessons learned
To glorify Christ in all we do.

"That the trial of your faith, being much more precious than of
gold that perisheth, though it be tried by fire, might be found unto
praise and honour and glory at the appearing of Jesus Christ."
(I Pet. 1:7)

THE WHOLE ARMOR

We are to put on the "Whole Armor of God,"
And having done so – stand,
As the forces of evil seek to destroy
God's work and perfect plan.
We gird ourselves with the "Truth" –
Christ Jesus – Lord of all;
And as our minds are stayed on Him,
We're safe whatever befall.
We put on the "Breastplate of Righteousness"
As we face the daily fight,
Shunning all the works of iniquity,
Standing for what is right.
Our feet are shod with the "Gospel of Peace"
As we walk on the battle ground,
Leaving footprints for others to follow,
That true peace would be found.
We take with us the "Shield of Faith,"
Trusting God each day –
Defense against the fiery darts
Satan sends our way.
We take the "Helmet of Salvation"
For protection of the mind –
A guard against all accusations,
And a witness to the spiritually blind.
We take the "Sword of the Spirit,"
Just as Moses took the rod;
It is the most powerful tool upon the earth –

The Word of The Living God.
When we wear this spiritual armor,
We're prepared for any battle that comes our way;
"No weapon formed against us shall prosper" –
God gives us victory every day.

"Wherefore take unto you the whole armour of God,
that ye may be able to withstand in the evil day,
and having done all, to stand."
"Thanks be to God, which giveth us the victory
through our Lord Jesus Christ."
(Eph. 6:13; I Cor. 15:57)

CHRIST'S RETURN

Christ is coming again in like manner
As the disciples saw Him go.
He's coming for His blood bought ones
Who watch and wait below.
Some would attempt to predict the day,
But no one knows just when,
Not even the angels in heaven,
Much less we mortal men.
Yet, as we discern the signs of the times,
We know His return is nigh;
Our glorious King is coming soon –
With a shout of the archangel on high.
The trumpet shall sound from heaven,
And the dead in Christ shall rise first;
Then those alive in Him shall be caught up –
No more suffering, hunger or thirst.
What a time of rejoicing it will be
When we meet our Lord in the air,
Singing hallelujahs – Glory to God,
Free from all trouble and care.
We mortals shall put on immortality
In the twinkling of an eye,
As we meet The King of Glory –
At that reunion in the sky.

Oh, what a glorious day that will be
When we see His wonderful face...
We'll praise Him throughout eternity
For His mercy and His grace.

"For the Lord himself shall descend from heaven with a shout,
with the voice of the archangel, and with the trump of God:
and the dead in Christ shall rise first:
Then we which are alive and remain shall be
caught up together with them in the clouds,
to meet the Lord in the air:
and so shall we ever be with the Lord."
(I Thes. 4:16-17)

THERE IS A RIVER

Whosoever drinks of the Water of Life
Shall never thirst again,
For within that soul's very being
Flows a river without end.
The middle wall of partition comes down
And the river rushes in,
With cleansing, healing water –
The broken heart to mend.
The streams make glad the city,
For God is in the midst,
And as the gentle water flows
The soul is filled with bliss.
Though the mountains tumble to the sea
And there's trouble all around,
That cool clear water is unmoved
And can evermore be found.
Praise God... There is a River,
Calm, peaceful and free,
To satisfy the thirsty soul
Through time and eternity.

"Whosoever drinketh of the water that I shall give him shall never thirst."
"There is a river, the streams whereof shall make glad the city of God...
God is in the midst of her; she shall not be moved."
(John 4:14; Ps. 46:4,5)

THIS GREAT NATION

Our Creator gives the beauty we see all about,
And also the freedom we enjoy throughout.
He holds This Great Nation in His hand
Working all things according to His plan.
His hand made America the best land of all,
One of great strength, upon which others call.
Many times we've extended a helping hand
For freedom and justice in another land.
Godly men have died these blessings to obtain,
And, oh, may their death never be in vain.
Let us live our lives standing for what's true,
Giving our best in all that we do;
And as we humbly walk before God in prayer,
Trusting, obeying, treating all men equal and fair,
Old Glory will wave high for all to see
We live in a land that truly is free;
And Lady Liberty shall continue to stand tall
Proclaiming This Nation – The Greatest of All!

"Blessed is the nation who's God is the Lord."
(Ps. 33:12)

141

OPPORTUNITY

Golden opportunities come our way,
Each and every one unique.
Doors and windows open wide
Through which God can speak.
As we closely follow the Shepherd
Through the open way,
We see His hand at work in others
As they hear what He would say.
Speaking through His Holy Word,
Giving directions so clear,
His Holy Spirit softens hearts,
Giving ears to hear.
What a privilege to view God's work
Through an open Opportunity;
Oh, may we never let a one go by
That could change a soul's destiny.
Father, give us courage to enter every window,
And walk through every door;
May hearts and souls be drawn to Thee
To live forevermore.

"Lift up your eyes and look on the fields;
for they are white already to harvest."
(John 4:35)

IN A ROSE

None could describe the beauty of a rose,
Nor the radiant splendor revealed as it grows –
But, oh, what a magnificent design!
As the delicate petals begin to unfold,
It speaks to the heart, lifting the soul –
A language beyond the mind.

So many travel life in the fast lanes
Missing the blessing a rose contains –
And such precious truths to glean!
But when one takes time to view this flower,
Reflected is the Designer's miraculous power –
And, oh, what a glory is seen...
In A Rose.

"The desert shall rejoice, and blossom as the rose.
It shall blossom abundantly, and rejoice
even with joy and singing...
they shall see the glory of the Lord,
and the excellency of our God."
(Isa. 35:1-2)

HOPE

In times of heartache, trouble, and sorrow,
Our precious Lord is there –
Strength for today – Hope for tomorrow,
Undergirding with love and care.
As our eyes are fixed on Him,
All fears within shall cease,
And we find beneath the suffering,
His joy and perfect peace.
As long as the moon shines at night
And the sun rises to light the day,
He still bestows mercy and grace
And hears us when we pray.
When we have God's grace
We can always cope,
And where His Spirit is
There is always Hope.

"Now the God of hope fill you with all joy and peace
in believing, that ye may abound in hope,
through the power of the Holy Ghost."
(Rom. 15:13)

TAKE A STAND

What a privilege has been ours to live in a nation
With biblical principles as it's foundation –
Blessings beyond measure.
May we have the courage to take a stand
Against the immorality now flooding our land –
Lest we lose this treasure.
Men pledged their lives, honor, fortunes and all,
Relying upon God's protection whatever befall,
For America to be free.
Oh, how we need to bow before God and pray
That these blessings not be taken away,
And that this land would always be:
"One nation under God... with liberty and justice for all."
Let us surrender our lives to the Holy Spirit's call,
Relying upon God's hand
For boldness to speak out against the sin
Destroying the foundations of this land...
God help us to Take A Stand!

"If thou shalt harken diligently unto the voice of the Lord thy God,
to observe and to do all his commandments... the Lord
thy God will set thee on high above all nations of the earth."
"Blessed shall thou be in the city and
blessed shall thou be in the field."
"The Lord shall open unto thee his good treasure."
(Deu. 28:1, 3, 12)

THE GLORY WOODS

The woods proclaim the glory of God...
Each leaf, each branch, each tree –
Lifting our hearts in praise to Him
For the many wonders we see.
The woodland animals all glorify Him,
Each and every frolicking one;
As we view God's creation and provision,
We rejoice in all He's done.
The deer, raccoons, squirrels, and rabbits
Bring glory to His name;
Even the chirping crickets and croaking frogs
All do the very same.
Each one of the birds of the air
Has its own praise to bring,
Gracefully soaring through the trees,
Freely and joyfully to sing.
When we're downhearted, feeling low,
With heavy burdens to bear,
We need only to walk among the trees...
God's presence is always there –
In The Glory Woods.

"Let the field be joyful, and all that is therein:
then shall all the trees of the wood rejoice before the Lord..."
"Blessed be his glorious name for ever:
and let the whole earth be filled with his glory."
(Ps. 96:12-13; 72:19)

BEYOND THE MIND

All who surrender to Christ shall find
Abundant blessings beyond the mind.
Within every believer there is wrought,
An intelligence beyond human thought –
A power beneath the weak mortal soul,
Forgiving, healing – making man whole.
Blinded eyes open... God's will to see;
Deaf ears hear... as the soul's set free.
A joyful fountain springs up in the heart
With a deep peace only God can impart.
A portion of heaven's blessings divine –
Spiritual life... Beyond The Mind!

"O the depth of the riches both of the
wisdom and knowledge of God!
How unsearchable are his judgments,
and his ways past finding out!"
(Rom. 11:33)

KINGDOM BUILDERS

"We are labourers together with God,"
United as sisters and brothers,
Spreading the Gospel Message –
Touching the lives of others.
Christ builds His Glorious Kingdom,
Stone upon precious stone,
As the Holy Spirit works in hearts,
Drawing them for His own.
Built upon The Solid Rock,
This house shall always stand,
Secure whatever storms may come –
God's gift to broken man.
Father, thank You for allowing us
To be laborers with Thee
As you reveal our Lord and King,
That others may be free.

"For we are labourers together with God:
ye are God's husbandry, ye are God's building."
"Ye also, as lively stones, are built up a spiritual house,
An holy priesthood, to offer up spiritual sacrifices,
acceptable to God by Jesus Christ."
(I Cor. 3:9; I Pet. 2:5)

SOLDIERS OF THE CROSS

We are soldiers of the cross,
Heeding the battle call;
Armed for spiritual warfare,
Standing firm and tall;
Lifting high God's banner,
His Spirit our shield and sword,
Bearing in our bodies,
The marks of our crucified Lord.
Following the risen Saviour,
Obeying His precious Word,
Shining the Light of the Gospel
Till all the world has heard.
Let us never be discouraged,
Though darker grows the night,
As Satan's time is running out,
Brighter glows the Light.
And when the battle here is ended,
With time on earth no more,
We'll celebrate the victory
On that bright celestial shore.

"Thou therefore endure hardness,
as a good soldier of Jesus Christ."
"Always bearing about in the body the dying of the Lord Jesus,
that the life also of Jesus might be made manifest in our body."
(II Tim. 2:3; II Cor. 4:10)

THE LIGHT OF HIS GLORY

The light of God's glory is seen
In the moon and each twinkling star;
The beauty of the sunrise and sunset –
A portion of heaven afar.
The trees and each magnificent flower,
The animals and birds of the air,
Declare the designer's mighty power,
And we know our God is there.
We stand in awe of His greatness
As we view all the beauty about;
Our souls bow down in silent worship
As our hearts rise up and shout;
For that same miraculous power
That created the wonders we see,
Touches the human heart and soul
Setting the prisoner free.
New creatures in Christ Jesus
Worship before the Throne,
Redeemed by the blood of the Lamb,
Purchased for His own.
God beautifies us with salvation,
Imparting spiritual life from above,
And we can see in one another
The Light of His Glory and love.

"Let your light so shine before men that they may see your good
works, and glorify your Father which is in heaven."
(Matt. 5:16)

GOD GIVE US ZEAL

Many are vulnerable and falling prey
To the false witnesses of our day.
Souls caught in the web of a cult's belief
Find only bondage, turmoil, and grief.
Oh, how we need passion and zeal
To take the message of Truth that's real
And boldly proclaim till all have heard
Of The Crucified Christ – The Living Word,
Resurrected by God's mighty power
To redeem souls this very hour.

God Give Us Zeal.

"Who gave himself for us, that he might redeem us from all iniquity,
and purify unto himself a peculiar people, zealous of good works."
(Tit. 2:14)

LIGHTER BURDENS

When we bear the burdens of another –
Suffering with our sister and brother,
Lifting them up in fervent prayer,
Lending a hand – showing we care,
Sharing their time of pain and sorrow,
Giving assurance of a better tomorrow,
Making their day just a little bit brighter...
We find our own burdens so much lighter.

"Bear ye one another's burdens,
and so fulfill the law of Christ."
(Gal. 6:2)

HE'S ALIVE

Christ Jesus is alive – Hallelujah! – He's Alive!
Lost souls to save, and others to revive –
Praise His Holy Name!
His touch changes lives, His love extends to all,
His mercy's for the guilty bowing to His call –
Thank God He came.
Oh, that we would never turn a deaf ear,
But always be ready and open to hear –
The Spirit's tender plea.
While many resist, reject and turn away
From His drawing power each day –
Let it not be you or me.
Father, tune the ears of our hearts, we pray,
To hear everything You would say –
Our wayward souls revive.
Help us to always be faithful and true
Following Christ in all that we do –
Hallelujah! – He's Alive!

"I am he that liveth, and was dead;
and behold, I am alive for evermore."
(Rev. 1:18)

GOD'S WAY IS BEST

Sometimes we earnestly, fervently pray,
Thinking we know what's best,
And receive something entirely different
From our petitions and requests.
Should we be discouraged or distraught
And think our Father hasn't heard?
Should we Listen to the adversary
Who'd have us doubt God's Word?
Satan delights in causing confusion,
Disturbing the peace in our souls,
But our loving Shepherd is faithful,
And our circumstances He controls.
Many times we've simply trusted
When we could not understand,
Always to find, further down the line,
It was best the way God planned.
He overrides our ignorant petitions,
And in spite of ourselves we find...
We are given exactly what we need
For a joyful life and peaceful mind.
Father, thank You for blessing us
By denying some requests.
Teach us to always trust You,
For we Know Your way is best.

"For my thoughts are not your thoughts, neither are
your ways my ways, saith the Lord."
"For as the heavens are higher than the earth, so are my ways
higher than your ways, and my thoughts than your thoughts."
(Isa. 55:8-9)

154

SOMEDAY

Someday there will be no more mountains to climb,
No more struggle or strife;
There will be no more dark valleys to walk through,
No more suffering in life.
Someday there will be no more burdens to bear,
No more heartache, trouble or sorrow;
There will be no more sickness or pain to endure,
For beyond the sunset is a new tomorrow.
Someday we'll depart for that promised land...
Hallellujah! What a a glorious place,
Forever to praise our God and King...
As we see Christ face to face.

Someday all who do not know Him as Lord
Shall stand before God's Throne,
There to give an account of their sinful deeds,
Forever reaping what they've sown.
Today seek His mercy, forgiveness, and grace
While His Spirit is calling you;
His love is plenteous, He'll forgive and pardon
And give you life anew.
"Someday" is so very near, my friend,
Oh, do not reject and turn away,
Call upon the Lord while He may be found...
Before the judgment day.

"Behold, now is the day of salvation."
"Whosoever shall call upon the name of the Lord shall be saved."
"For thou, Lord, art good, and ready to forgive;
and plenteous in mercy unto all them that call upon thee."
(II Cor. 6:2; Rom. 10:13; Ps. 86:5)

155

IN HIS SIGHT

Whatsoever our hand finds to do,
Let us do it with all our might,
Not for the vain praise of men,
But because we're In God's Sight.
The loving eye of our Holy Father
Sees every thought and deed,
And His hand is always ready
To guide and meet our need.
Oh, how we desire to please Him
And be all He'd have us be,
For He gave His all on Calvary
To redeem you and me.
How could we not fervently serve
With all our strength and might?
Hallellujah! – He is with us,
We're always – In His Sight!

Lord, help us to serve You heartily
In all we say and do,
For our hearts' greatest desire
Is to please and glorify You.

"And whatsoever ye do, do it heartily, as to the Lord, and not
unto men; knowing that of the Lord ye shall receive the reward
of the inheritance; for ye serve the Lord Christ."
(Col. 3:23-24)

THE GOOD SHEPHERD

The Good Shepherd always walks in front,
Gently leading the way,
Never behind driving or pushing,
But lovingly guiding each day;
And when a sheep wanders away
From the security of this place,
The Shepherd corrects the wayward one
In love, mercy, and grace.
He protects from harm and fear
All that follow His lead;
His rod and staff guard and comfort,
And His hand meets every need.
He provides beautiful green pastures –
Rest for the weary and weak,
Revival, strength and vigor...
Peace and joy to reap.
He sets a table in the wilderness
With manna from on high,
And leads beside the still waters
That refresh and satisfy.
Oh, what love and tender care,
Such blessings God bestows
Upon the sheep that closely follow...
The way The Shepherd goes.

Jesus said: "I am the good Shepherd,
and know my sheep, and am known of mine."
"My sheep hear my voice, and I know them, and they follow me."
(John 10:14, 27)

PROSPERITY

It's not adversity
That clouds our spiritual view,
But rather prosperity,
And the vain pleasures we pursue.
We go through hardship
With our focus on God above,
But earthly possessions
Can cause us to forget His love.
May we never have so much
Of this world's goods and treasure,
That we lose site of the Giver
Of true wealth beyond measure.

"Feed me with food convenient for me;
Lest I be full, and deny Thee,
and say, Who is the LORD?"
(Pro. 30:8-9)

KNOWLEDGE IS BLISS

Ignorance is never bliss
In the things of eternity,
For knowledge of the Truth
Sets repentant souls free;
Free from darkness, fear,
And restlessness within;
Free to live righteously
As God forgives all sin.
To know Christ is bliss…
Such peace and joy abound;
Surrendering all to Him…
Abundant life is found.
This knowledge of Truth
Must not be missed,
For He's the only way
To everlasting bliss.

"And ye shall know the truth,
and the truth shall make you free."
(John 8:32)

REVIVAL

God gives revival every day
As we look to Him in Prayer,
Wherever we may be
His Holy Spirit's there –
The Great Almighty God,
Yet our dearest, closest Friend,
As He communes with us
Our hearts are stirred within.
No man can bring revival,
Nor can it be worked up;
Only God can touch a heart,
And fill an empty cup.
Whether in the deepest valley,
Or on the mountain high,
Revival comes from God alone
As souls to Him draw nigh.
It may be in the morning,
Or in the noonday bright;
It may be in a crowded place,
Or alone in the darkest night;
It may be in a warm, loving church
Where spiritual blessings flow,
Or behind cold prison walls
Where no spiritual life doth show.

God's hand is always extended,
No matter where we are,
To draw closely back to Himself
Souls who've wandered afar.
Revival's for those alive in Christ
Who've gone their selfish way...
Oh, how we all need Revival
Each and every day.
Father, give us contrite hearts,
As we humbly bow and pray.

"Wilt thou not revive us again:
that thy people may rejoice in thee?"
"Create in me a clean heart, O God;
and renew a right spirit within me."
(Ps. 85:6; 51:10)

SALVATION

To be apart from Christ is death –
No spiritual life to revive;
His precious blood made the way
For souls to come alive:
Totally and completely dead,
Mere clay on earthly sod,
The seed of faith lies dormant
Till touched by the living God...
Hallelujah! A new creature's created,
As grace and faith unite,
Miraculously... deaf ears hear,
Blind eyes receive their sight,
A fountain of joy springs up within
Filling the thirsty soul,
And the angels of heaven rejoice...
A sinner is made whole.

Praise God for His great Salvation!

"By grace are ye saved through faith; and that not of yourselves:
it is the gift of God: not of works, lest any man should boast."
"There is joy in the presence of the angels of God
over one sinner that repenteth."
(Ephes. 2:8,9; Luke 15:10)

A SPIRITUAL GAUGE

God gives a gauge for testing
Actions, words, and intentions,
Attitudes and motivations,
All beliefs and opinions;
It's a useful tool for determining
Where a person stands –
The heart's moral fiber,
The work of the hands;
It protects from sin and error,
Keeping the soul on track,
And should one get off,
It's a compass pointing back.
This gauge is a mere simple question,
Reading: "yes" or "no;"
All should use it every day,
Wherever they may go.
Question: "Does it glorify Christ?"
If "no" – from it depart...
If "yes" – support it
With all your heart.

Thank God, His Holy Spirit
reveals truth and error.

Christ said: "Howbeit when he, the spirit of truth is come,
he will guide you into all truth... He shall glorify me."
(John 16:13-14)

THE NEED WITHIN

There's a need within each heart
Only God can supply;
A thirst within each soul
Only He can satisfy;
A restlessness and hunger
Nothing else can fill;
Only Christ can meet the need,
And whisper "peace be still."
Some try to fill the emptiness
With so many other things,
Never knowing the blessing
The Holy Spirit brings;
Oh the terrible tragedy
Of this eternal loss,
When such joyful blessings flow
At the foot of the cross.

Father, thank You
For supplying the need within,
As we come to know Christ,
And forgiveness of sin.

"For he satisfieth the longing soul,
and filleth the hungry soul with goodness."
(Ps. 107:9)

Faith Messages IV

"We are the people of his pasture,
and the sheep of his hand."
(Psalms 95:7)

Faith IV

Seek Ye First

WHAT TO SEEK

Let us not seek...
How close to the world we can live
And still be God's own...
What a Loss!

But let us seek...
How close to God we can live
That He be more fully known...
What a Gain!

"If ye then be risen with Christ,
seek those things which are above,
where Christ sitteth on the right hand of God.
Set your affection on things above,
not on things on the earth."
"When Christ, who is our life shall appear,
then shall ye also appear with him in glory."
(Col. 3:1-2, 4)

THE WRITTEN WORD

The Bible, God's Holy Written Word,
Is His message to all mankind –
The book of law and guidance
For the heart, soul and mind.
It's so much more than a history book,
Though all accounts are true,
It's a personal letter from our loving Father,
Written specifically for me and you.
A letter of mercy and tenderness,
One of unconditional love and grace;
It tells of the sacrificial death of His Son,
For every kindred, tongue and race.
God inspired the precious message
The pen of man wrote down,
And whenever it's pages are opened
Manna from heaven is found.
Hungry, seeking souls are fed
Reading the Word each day,
As the Holy Spirit illumines truth,
Revealing God's will and way.
The Author is His own interpreter
For the open, thirsty heart,
And the water of life flows freely
To saturate every part.
When it's difficult to comprehend
The contents of His letter,
If we'll draw closer to the Author...
We'll understand it better.

Father, thank You for The Written Word –
Our instruction book for life;
It's an anchor that always holds
In the storms of trouble and strife.

"All scripture is given by inspiration of God."
"For the prophecy came not in old time
by the will of man: but holy men of God
spake as they were moved by the Holy Ghost."
(II Tim. 3:16; II Pet. 1:21)

THE LIVING WORD

The Living Word unlocks the heart,
He holds the only key,
And as the door is opened,
The captive is set free.
The Word that was with God
Before the world began,
Left His home in glory
To redeem fallen man.
Made flesh to dwell among us,
Full of truth and grace,
In Him was life, the light of men,
Shining from His face...
The sacrificial Lamb to be slain –
Without one blemish or spot,
The Light in darkness – the Son of God,
Yet the world knew Him not.
All were bound by darkness and fear,
No hope of life within,
But the chains fell off as He arose...
Freeing His people from sin.
Man could not kill The Living Word,
He's alive in hearts today –
God's perfect law now fulfilled
As believers walk His way.

Father, thank You for The Living Word
That sets our spirit free,
And lights our lives from above...
As we surrender all to Thee.

"And the Word was made flesh, and dwelt among us,
and we beheld his glory, the glory as of
the only begotten of the father, full of grace and truth."
"In him was life; and the life was the light of men."
(John 1:14, 4)

I STAND AMAZED

I stand amazed at the goodness of God,
His mercy and mighty power,
His compassion and tender loving care,
His presence in the darkest hour.
Amazed at His comfort in times of grief,
His strength in the hardest day,
Sufficient grace in the time of need,
Forgiveness when we go astray.
Amazed when He calms the angry storm,
Even more at the peace in the midst,
The secure anchor that always holds,
Giving underlying joy and bliss.
Amazed, not just when He grants a request,
But when He protects by denying a plea,
And those times when He has us wait,
More grace than ever we see.
Nothing is too hard for the God we serve,
By His power He sets us free;
I Stand Amazed, not at what He can do…
But that He would do it for me.

"I will praise thee, O Lord my God, with all my heart:
and I will glorify thy name forevermore."
(Ps. 86:12)

SERVE GOD TODAY

This is the day the Lord hath made,
So swiftly it's passing by;
Signs of the times are very clear,
Redemption draweth nigh.
Are we doing all we can today,
Serving our God and King?
Have we any gifts of sacrifice
Before His throne to bring?
When His kingdom shall unveil
With Glory from the sky,
Will we be ready to meet Him
In His holiness on high?
The day of His coming is so near,
It's sovereignly arranged;
We must work while there is time,
And lives can still be changed.
Nothing's ever done tomorrow,
Or in the yesterday;
One's a vision, the other a dream...
We must Serve God Today.

"Serve the Lord with gladness."
"Exhort one another daily, while it is called To day."
"Labour not for the meat which perisheth,
but for that meat which endureth unto everlasting life."
(Ps. 100:2; Heb. 3:13; John 6:27)

A BURDEN FOR SOULS

Our hearts are heavily burdened
For souls in a faraway place,
Who've never heard the preaching
Of God's amazing grace;
But, a message is in the sunset,
The moon and stars above,
Declaring the creator's goodness,
Mercy, grace and love.
A native in a distant land
Told a missionary who came:
"I know the One of Whom you speak,
I just didn't know His name."
Nature itself bears witness
Of God's mighty power and Truth,
As the Holy Spirit, Himself, teaches,
All men are without excuse.
An even greater burden
Is for those who hear the Word,
And go their sinful way
As though they'd never heard.
Having ears to hear, they hear not
What the Spirit would say,
Rejecting Christ the Saviour,
Refusing to bow and pray.

It's a greater burden we carry,
For it's a greater price they'll pay
When they meet the Lord of Glory
On that Judgment Day.

Father, help us to obey the great commission
Taking the message to all,
May we be sensitive to Your lead,
And hear Your Spirit's call.

"Today if ye will hear his voice, harden not your hearts."
"Blessed are they that hear the word of God, and keep it."
(Heb. 4:7; Luke 11:28)

THE LIVING CHURCH

The true church is alive and well,
Not made with mortal hands,
But, built by the great Designer,
According to His plans.
Resting upon the solid Rock,
The only safe foundation,
The church is strong and secure,
Without sin's degradation.
Constructed not with wood or hay,
Nor with silver or fine gold,
But, with precious lively stones,
Chosen and sealed to hold...
Stones made righteous and holy,
Serving the maker as priests,
Offering spiritual sacrifices
And praises without cease.
Though forceful winds and rains
Batter the house with hail,
The Rock, the Chief Cornerstone,
Holds firm within the vale.
The work will soon be complete,
The last stone put in place;
Hallelujah!... The Living Church
Shall meet the Builder face to face.

"Ye also, as lively stones, are built up a spiritual house, a holy priesthood,
to offer up spiritual sacrifices, acceptable to God by Jesus Christ."
(I Peter 2:5)

A SIMPLE MESSAGE

Nothing's complicated about the cross,
And God's redemption plan;
The message is so pure and simple
Even a child can understand.
It doesn't take a learned theologian,
An intellectual, or a degree,
To comprehend what took place
On that old rugged tree;
For the Truth is not a complex one,
As to some it doth appear,
It's not entangled or confused,
But, direct and very clear.
God gave His only begotten Son
To pardon and set free,
And each precious drop of blood
Was shed for you and me.
It doesn't take a bible scholar
To explain conviction;
A soul brought low by sin and guilt
Experiences the affliction.
As God forgives, revealing Christ,
Making the sinner whole,
That new and glorious life imparted
Is felt within the soul.
But, to all who reject and believe not,
This Truth is concealed,
Such as with those who questioned
The blind man healed;
Miraculously touched, he understood,
For his spirit was set free,
And the answer he gave was simple:
"I once was blind, but now I see."
It's A Simple Message.

"But if our gospel be hid, it is hid to them that are lost: In whom the
god of this world hath blinded the minds of them which believe not,
lest the light of the glorious gospel of Christ,
who is the image of God, should shine unto them."
(II Cor. 4:3-4)

THE SOLID ROCK

As our souls cry out for mercy
In a dry and thirsty land,
We're led to the solid Rock
By God's omnipotent hand.
Lovingly lifting us from the pit
Of murky, miry clay,
He sets our feet upon the Rock,
Establishing our way.
No longer living in darkness,
The light of Glory unfolds,
For the spiritual Rock of ages
Now lives within our souls.
Joyful praise is upon our lips,
A new song in our hearts,
Hidden in the cleft of the Rock,
Are treasures God imparts.
The Living water flows freely
Satisfying every need,
And the bread of life is abundant
Our hungry souls to feed.
We're safe and secure forever –
Sheltered in the flock,
For our feet are firmly planted
On Christ – The Solid Rock.

"He brought me up also out of an horrible pit, out of the miry clay,
and set my feet upon a rock, and established my goings.
And he put a new song in my mouth, even praise unto our God."
(Ps. 40:2-3)

PRAY AND OBEY

Bowing before the Throne of Grace
In earnest humble prayer,
Our innermost needs are satisfied
As our Saviour meets us there.
The turbulent storms may not cease,
The valleys may still be deep,
But, God's grace is all sufficient –
His joyous blessing we reap.
Let us pray not for an easy road,
Free from trouble and care,
Lest we should stray from our Lord,
And miss the blessing there;
But, let us pray for a righteous heart,
One pure and clean within –
Revived and ready to serve our God,
Forgiven of all known sin.
Then let us pray for one another,
And diligently intercede,
When the righteous fervently pray,
God hears and meets the need.
Let us bow in prayer for our nation
And all who lead and serve,
Many have sacrificed their lives
Our freedoms to preserve;
And let us pray for the world abroad,
Hearing the desperate cry –
So much hunger and suffering,
We dare not pass them by.
Let us obey the great commission,
Sharing the gospel with all,
As we walk in fellowship with God,
Responding to His call;
For there's no other way to prepare
For that Judgment Day,
Than to meet and follow the Master
As we Pray And Obey.

"Pray without ceasing."
"The effectual fervent prayer of a righteous man availeth much."
"Behold, to obey is better than sacrifice."
(I Thes. 5:17; Jas. 5:16; I Sam. 15:22)

179

THE HOLY LIGHT

As we see the Light from heaven,
And our sin He willingly bore,
Our hearts cry out for mercy...
And the darkness is no more.
He's our sunshine in the daytime,
The moon and stars at night;
The fire within our heart and soul
Forever burning bright.
He lights our lives with goodness,
His glory shines right through,
Touching the lives of others
As His will we humbly do.
No other light's so powerful,
None other can thrill our soul,
Nor penetrate the darkness
Making the sinner whole.
No other fire can melt the dross
Formed within the heart,
Nor purify the repentant one,
Cleansing every part.
Praise God for The Holy Light,
The One who's faithful and true,
The Flame within our being...
That gives us life anew.

"In him was life; and the life was the light of men."
(John 1:4)

THE HOLY SPIRIT

We may hear choice preachers
Expound God's written Word,
But, unless the Holy Spirit teaches,
It's as though we'd never heard.
He gives light to darkened hearts,
And sight to blinded eyes,
And the precious Truth He imparts
Is eternally realized.
He never speaks of Himself
As He functions here on earth,
But draws lost souls to Christ,
Repentance, and new birth.
He's the One sent by our Lord
To comfort, teach, and Guide,
Entering our hearts at salvation
Forevermore to abide.
He's the third person of the Trinity,
Equal with the Father and Son;
Each have different functions,
Yet, our God is One.
The Holy Spirit can be blasphemed,
Rejected, quenched, and grieved;
Or He can be heard and followed,
Submitted to, and received.
Father, help us to depart from evil,
And all known sin,
As we learn to listen to The Holy Spirit –
Your still, small voice within.

"For there are three that bear record in heaven, The Father,
the Word, and the Holy Ghost: and these three are one."
Jesus said: "And I will pray the Father, and he shall give you another
Comforter, that he may abide with you for ever;
... he dwelleth with you, and shall be in you."
"The Comforter, which is the Holy Ghost, whom the
Father will send in my name, he shall teach you all things."
"He will guide you into all truth... He shall glorify me."
(I John 5:7; John 14:16, 17, 26; 16:13, 14)

181

THOSE SPECIAL BLESSINGS

Praise God for those special blessings
He sends along life's way –
The times of revival and renewal
When excitement fills the day.
In these mountain top experiences
We clearly hear His voice,
And our souls are filled with vigor,
As our yielded hearts rejoice.
Working in our lives, and others,
The Light of His Glory shines,
And we joyfully sing His praises
During these special times.
But, let us never fail to praise Him
For His sustaining power
That keeps us steady in the boat
Through the stormy hour.
Those times we feel we're sinking
In the ocean of dark despair,
A still voice quietly whispers peace,
And we know our Lord is there.
As He walks with us through the valley,
He seems closer than before –
The darker the night, the brighter the Light,
His Glory shines even more.

Then, when there are no highs or lows,
But, merely a routine day,
Those Special Blessings still fill our souls
Every step of the way.

"Blessed be the God and Father of our Lord Jesus Christ,
who hath blessed us with all spiritual blessings
in heavenly places in Christ."
(Eph. 1:3)

GRADUATION DAY

Graduation Day is coming –
We shall leave this training place,
Receiving the highest degree,
As we behold His wondrous face.
Hallelujah! What a glorious day –
Our souls completely free
To dwell with Christ, our Saviour,
Through all eternity.
Rewards shall be bestowed
At His judgment seat,
But the greatest one of all
Shall be to sit at His feet.
Until then, let us do our best
To follow His will and way,
Obeying the inner promptings,
As He instructs and leads each day.
Time is of the essence,
So swiftly it's fleeting by,
Let us worship God in all we do
Till we reach our home on high.
Father, forgive us when we fail you,
Teach us to hear and obey,
Train our wayward hearts,
For Graduation Day.

"Thus saith the Lord, thy Redeemer, the Holy One of Israel;
I am the Lord thy God which teacheth thee to profit,
which leadeth thee by the way that thou shouldest go."
"And his servants shall serve him: And they shall see his face."
(Is. 48:17; Rev. 22:3-4)

GOD'S LOVE

The love among God's people
Reaches from heart to heart,
With an unconditional caring
Only Christ can impart
Not a product of mortal man,
But of the Living Word,
Without it, mere sounding brass
And tinkling cymbals are heard.
The very first fruit of the Spirit –
The first and greatest command:
"Love God with all your heart,
And then your fellow man."
Only because He first loved us,
Can we love our Lord at all,
The shed blood on Calvary
Broke down the middle wall.
Love's the fulfilling of the law,
There is no other way,
But to walk in the Holy Spirit,
Bearing His fruit each day.
Oh, what blessings bestowed
Within the believer's soul –
The warm flame of God's Love...
Never shall grow cold.

"The love of God is shed abroad in our hearts
by the Holy Ghost which is given unto us."
(Rom. 5:5)

FELLOWSHIP DIVINE

To know Him is to love Him –
Sweet Fellowship Divine;
He speaks peace to our hearts,
And such joy in Him we find.
As He closely walks beside us,
His Spirit fills our souls,
And when we need Him most,
Our feeble hands He holds.
We need no other counselor,
We need no other guide...
Our Shepherd, the Comforter,
Is always by our side.
Sheltered safely in His care
Till we reach heaven's shore,
Oh, what Fellowship Divine...
Now and forevermore.

Father, thank You that in Christ
We have fellowship with Thee,
May it always be unbroken
Through time and eternity.

"And truly our fellowship is with the Father,
and with his Son Jesus Christ."
(I John 1:3)

CHRISTIAN FELLOWSHIP

Oh, what sweet communion
In God's only Son;
Loving Christian fellowship –
Hearts united as one;
Joined together in Christ,
Free from the state of sin,
Adoring the King of kings –
Our very closest Friend.
One common purpose,
And one single goal –
To glorify our Saviour
Till heavens gates unfold.

Lord, thank You for Christian Fellowship
Uniting our hearts in love;
We pray You'd keep us ever close,
Till we reach our home above.

"If we walk in the light, as he is in the light,
we have fellowship one with another,
and the blood of Jesus Chirst his Son
cleanseth us from all sin."
(I John 1:7)

HOW MANY TIMES

How many times have we closed our ears
To what our Lord would say,
Turned our backs to the call of God,
And gone our selfish way?
How many times have we shut our eyes
To Truth so plain and clear,
And stubbornly remained in our sins
When His Spirit drew us near?
How many times have we clinched our hand
And denied a friend in need,
Failing to reach out in love and give,
With a kind, unselfish deed?
How many times have we walked on by
A troubled, hurting brother,
Too busy to care, and have compassion,
Too preoccupied to help another?
God, forgive us for the many times
We've failed to follow You;
Help us to be sensitive and caring,
And always ask: "What would Jesus do?"

"Then said Jesus unto his disciples, If any man will come after me,
let him deny himself, and take up his cross, and follow me.
For whosoever will save his life shall lose it:
And whosoever will lose his life for my sake shall find it."
(Matt. 16:24-25)

LIBERTY

Give me Christ or give me death!
He's more than life to me.
Hearts surrendered to the Master
Find true Liberty.

"Where the spirit of the Lord is, there is liberty."
"Stand fast therefore in the liberty
wherewith Christ hath made us free,
and be not entangled again with the yoke of bondage."
(II Cor. 3:17; Gal. 5:1)

SEEK THE LORD

Oh, sinner, seek the Lord
With all your heart and soul;
Seek forgiveness, mercy and grace –
See the blessings of God unfold.

Oh, Christian, seek the Lord
With all your heart and soul;
Seek to follow Christ and do His will –
See the blessings of God unfold.

"Seek ye the Lord while he may be found,
call ye upon him while he is near:"
"Seek ye first the kingdom of God, and his righteousness,
and all these things shall be added unto you."
(Is. 55:6; Matt. 6:33)

WHEN WE FAIL

Our loving Lord doesn't judge us
For every mistake we make,
But gently guides our steps
In the paths we should take;
And when we stumble in our walk,
Our Shepherd's hand is there,
Ready to correct, comfort, and lead
In love, and tender care.
His vision is always perfectly clear
When ours is foggy and dim,
And When We Fail along the way...
We learn to depend on Him.

Lord, thank you for loving us
Though we are weak and frail,
Teach us to depend more on You,
And forgive us when we fail.

"We have this treasure in earthen vessels,
that the excellency of the power
may be of God, and not of us."
(II Cor. 4:7)

191

PEACE AND JOY AT CHRISTMAS

The peace that passes understanding,
And joy that last all year,
Are not found in wrapped packages,
Bright lights or Christmas cheer,
But in the quietness of the spirit
Humbly submitted and still,
As one comes to know the Saviour,
His purpose and His will.
He's more than a babe in a manger,
More than a Christmas story;
He's the Son of The Living God...
The Eternal King of Glory.
The wondrous light of His presence
Gives true joy all year round,
And as He indwells His people...
It's there real peace is found.
As we celebrate His miracle birth
This busy time of year,
May we truly worship our Lord
And sense His presence near.
May our hearts be filled with praise
To Christ our Lord and King,
For the everlasting Peace and Joy...
Knowing Him doth bring.

"For He is our peace."
"Believing, ye rejoice with joy unspeakable and full of glory."
(Ephes. 2:14; I Pet. 1:8)

HIS VOLUNTARY DEATH

The crown of thorns upon His head,
The nails driven in His hands,
Each precious drop of blood He shed...
Ordained by His own plans.
The spikes forced through His holy feet,
The sword pierced through His side,
Such agony He suffered there...
Willingly for His bride.
The ridicule and mocking of His name,
The marring of His brilliant face,
The ugly death of a sinner's shame...
As He hung there in our place.
The prophesied Messiah, the sinless One,
The sacrificial Lamb so pure,
The Miracle Worker who raised the dead...
Gave Himself, salvation to procure.
No man could take His life from Him,
For none could stay His hand;
Jesus, omnipotent God in the flesh...
Voluntarily died for man.

Jesus said: "I lay down my life for the sheep."
"No man taketh it from me but I lay it down of myself.
I have power to lay it down, and I have power to take it again."
(John 10:15, 18)

HOPE FOR MAN

As long as the day breaks and the cock crows,
The songbirds awake and the river flows,
God still has a plan.
As long as the sun rises in the sky above,
And the moon and stars shout His love,
There's still Hope For Man.

"For thou art my hope, O Lord God."
"Happy is he that hath the God of Jacob for his help,
whose hope is in the Lord his God."
(Ps. 71:5; 146:5)

OUR HEAVIEST BURDENS

The burdens we don't understand
Are the heaviest to bear,
But rested in God's sovereign hand...
They're so much lighter there.
When we simply trust our Lord
With what's beyond our sight,
Lovingly, He lifts the weight...
As He works it all out right.

"Cast thy burden upon the Lord,
and He shall sustain thee."
(Ps. 55:22)

OUR LORD'S WITH US

Upon the highest mountain,
Or in the valley low,
Our Shepherd walks beside us
Wherever we go.
Over dry barren land,
Or through rough waters deep,
His hand's there to guide us,
To comfort and keep.
And in dark troublesome times
When danger surrounds,
His sheltering wings hide us
On heavenly grounds.
More love and mercy revealed,
More grace to carry on,
After He has tried us,
Making Himself known.
Eternal victory's ours
Following His lead...
For His Spirit lives inside us,
Our hungry souls to feed.

"Ye shall know Him; for he dwelleth
with you and shall be in you."
(John 14:17)

HUMBLE STILL

Humbly – we bow before the cross,
Seeking forgiveness there,
Where Christ suffered, bled and died...
All our sins to bear.
Humbly – we receive God's pardon,
Believing in Him who came,
Gloriously freed from bondage...
We praise His Holy Name.
Humbly – we sit at our Saviour's feet,
Worshipping His Majesty,
Abundantly reaping from that seat...
The blessings of eternity.
Humbly – we walk before our God,
Following our Shepherd's lead,
Gladly hearing the Spirit's call...
His Holy Word to heed.
Fervently we serve our Lord and King,
Joyfully doing His will,
Living in His grace and power...
He keeps us Humble Still.

"God resisteth the proud,
but giveth grace to the humble."
(James 4:6)

GOD'S KINGDOM IS AT HAND

God's great kingdom is entered
Right here upon the earth,
As we come to know the Saviour
In the glorious new birth.
Abundant life in Christ begins
When the Holy Seed's conceived –
Heaven comes down and joy springs up
As the Son of God's received.
Rich spiritual blessings fill our souls
Each day we serve our King,
And though all around may tumble down,
In the midst our hearts can sing.
No need to wait for the pearly gate
To rejoice in the promised land –
Hallelujah! A portion abides in us here...
God's Kingdom Is At Hand.

"The time is fulfilled, and the kingdom of God
is at hand: repent ye, and believe the gospel."
"God is the strength of my heart, and my portion for ever."
(Mark 1:15; Ps. 73:26)

PRECIOUS GIFTS

Brothers and Sisters in Christ
Who enrich the heart and soul
Are precious gifts from God
More valuable than pure gold!

"My fruit is better than gold,
yea, than fine gold."
(Pr. 8:19)

ASK NOT

Ask not what your Saviour can do for you...
Consider the old rugged tree;
Now ask what you can do for Him,
Your soul having been set free.
Surrendered before The Throne of Grace,
Having humbly bowed to pray...
Arise to serve your God and King
And live for Him each day.

Ask not what your neighbor can do for you
As you walk this pilgrim land,
But what you can do along life's way
To help your fellowman.
It's not in receiving the finest gifts
That rich treasure is found,
But in the deeds you do for others
As you share God's love around.

Ask not what your church can do for you
To supply your every need,
But what you can do for the ministry
In spreading the gospel seed.
When you take the message of the Master
And share it in all you do...
Bountiful blessings without number
Come right back home to you.

"Give, and it shall be given unto you; good measure, pressed down,
and shaken together, and running over, shall men give into your bosom.
For with the same measure that ye mete with all
it shall be measured to you again."
(Luke 6:38)

DARKNESS SHALL FLEE

The darkness shall never dispel the Light,
Though it's forces continually try,
More powerful is The Son of God...
The eternal Light from on high.
Radiating in and through His people
To set the captives free,
Every place that glorious Light touches...
All darkness and fear doth flee.

Jesus said: "I am the Light of the world:
He that followeth me shall not walk in darkness,
but shall have the Light of life."
(John 8:12)

PARADOXICAL TRUTHS

Truly Seeing – we believe
Truly Believing – we see...
As God sets our spirit free.

Graciously Giving – we receive
Graciously Receiving – we give...
As God teaches us how to live.

To Step Up – we must step down
Stepping Down – God lifts us up...
As He fills our spiritual cup.

To Live – we must die to self
In Dying to Self - we're made alive ...
God's Glory to derive.

"To Live – is Christ
To Die – is gain..."
Forevermore with Him to reign!

"Who hath ears to hear, let him hear."
"It is given unto you to know the mysteries
of the kingdom of heaven."
(Matt. 13:9, 11)

THE LORD WILL MAKE A WAY... SOMEHOW

When you come to the end of your pathway
To an ocean of shattered dreams,
And wonder how you could travel on –
No hope at all it seems,
Just remember the Hebrew children,
Somehow that sea did part...
Hallelujah! God made a path for them,
And He'll mend your broken heart.

When you come to the end of your resource,
And you know not what to do,
Just look to the God of the universe,
He'll meet that need for you.
Remember the widow's little oil,
Somehow it never ran dry...
Hallelujah! Her every need was met
By the Lord's endless supply.

When you come to the end of your..self,
And you feel your life is o'er,
Surrender your all to the Son of God,
He'll bless you forevermore.
Just remember Paul's conversion
On that Damascus road...
Hallelujah! God touched his life that day
And forever lifted his load.

When you come to the end of your sin,
So broken, helpless and lost,
There's a Saviour ready to pardon you,
As He did the thief on the cross.
The Holy, Righteous Son of God
Hung beside him on a tree...
Hallelujah! He took his sin away
And set that captive free.

The Lord will make a way... somehow;
Somehow He'll carry you through.
What He did back then He will do again...
He will somehow make a way for you.

"Jesus Christ the same yesterday, and to day and for ever."
(Heb. 13:8)

STRONG FAITH

Many have... No Faith – having never heard
Many others... Little Faith – knowing little of God's Word
A few have... Much Faith – nurturing the Word
they receive
Even fewer... STRONG FAITH – willing to die
for what they believe.

Father, we know You give grace in time of need,
But strengthen within our hearts, even now, faith's seed.
Help us to know, if faced with the enemy's gun or sword,
We'd have STRONG FAITH and not deny our Lord.

"Faith cometh by hearing,
and hearing by the word of God."
(Rom. 10:17)

THE LIGHT OF CALVARY

Lifted from a dark domain...
Into Thy marvelous Light,
Delivered from a state of sin –
Given new spiritual sight,
The pleasures of this world are nothing
Compared, oh, Lord to Thee,
As a heart, once dark and blind,
Sees the Light of Calvary.
Not a trace of desire to go back,
For this world holds no attraction,
Walking in Thy Light we find
Complete joy and satisfaction.
Wondrous pleasures enrich our lives
In the realm of true reality...
As such glorious blessings unfold
In the Light of Calvary.

"Ye were sometimes darkness,
but now are ye light in the Lord:
walk as children of the light:
(For the fruit of the Spirit is in all goodness
and righteousness and truth)."
(Eph. 5:8-9)

HE'LL TAKE CARE OF YOU

God made the earth, and all within,
The rolling sea, and mortal men,
He is our God, and He'll take care of you.

He hung the moon in outer space,
And put each star in its own place,
The mighty God can sure take care of you.

He gave His Son on Calv'rys tree
To save from sin and set you free,
Our loving Lord has made a way for you.

He'll be your guide in all you do,
He'll take your hand and lead you through,
He is your God, and He'll Take Care of You.

"Humble yourselves therefore under the mighty hand of God,
that he may exalt you in due time:
Casting all your care upon him; for he careth for you."
"In all thy ways acknowlege him, and he shall direct thy paths."
(I Pet. 5:6-7; Prov. 3:6)

ANGELS UNAWARE

You never know as you meet someone
Just what might be their need.
Sometimes a warm smile or handshake
Is all it takes to plant a fruitful seed.
Other times you may need to speak a word
Of encouragement to a sister or brother,
Or share your faith along the way
As God gives opportunity with another.
When you meet with a hurting neighbor
Along side of your journey's road,
Be sure to reach out with a loving hand
And help carry their heavy load;
For you never know on life's pathway
Just who you might meet there...
Always take note of each precious soul,
For some have entertained Angels Unaware.

"Let brotherly love continue.
Be not forgetful to entertain strangers:
for thereby some have entertained angels unaware."
(Heb. 13:1-2)

A TWO WAY STREET

When we come before God's Throne
In special time of prayer,
So often we do all the talking...
Never hearing from heaven there.
Perhaps we're in a hurry,
Or just totally unaware...
It's A Two Way Street
When we come to God in prayer.

When we're still and quiet before God,
He speaks to our hearts,
Instructing, guiding, empowering...
As His message He imparts.
May we always remember
When unloading all our care...
It's A Two Way Street
When we come to God in prayer.

"I will hear what God the Lord will speak:
for he will speak peace unto his people, and to his saints:
but let them not turn again to folly."
"Cause me to hear thy loving kindness in the morning;
for in thee do I trust: cause me to know the way
wherein I should walk; for I lift up my soul unto thee."
(Ps. 85:8; 143:8)

THE SOLUTION

Let us always be very careful
When we have a legitimate concern.
Remember the Lord is there to guide
When in prayer to Him we turn.
An evil report given
Is such a destructive force,
But problems become opportunities
When taken to the right source.
Our Lord is the Master of circumstance,
He can turn it all around,
As we trust and rely on Him
The right solution is found.
So, rather than spreading an evil report,
Take your concern to God in prayer,
Then follow His guiding hand...
You'll find The Solution there.

"Praying always with all prayer and supplication in the Spirit,
and watching thereunto with all perseverance
and supplication for all saints."
(Eph. 6:18)

CONFORMING TO HIS IMAGE

This mortal could never be
Like God's holy, righteous Son,
For within is no good thing,
"None is righteous, no not one."
Thank God for the new birth –
Christ's Spirit living within,
Enabling us to follow Him,
Free from lust and sin.
We're conformed to His image
As we read God's Holy Word,
Obeying His will and way –
His precious truths having heard;
As we grow in grace we find
His Spirit in us increased,
And our fleshly mortal self,
Has now, somehow, decreased.
As we walk in His Spirit,
Our own flesh made weak,
God conforms us to His image
As His holiness we seek.

"He must increase, but I must decrease."
"Yield your members servants
to righteousness unto holiness."
(John 3:30; Rom. 6:19)

TAKE ALL WE ARE

Take all we are, all we have,
And all we hope to be...
Use us, Dear Lord, each day we live
To bring glory and honor to Thee.
This world is not our home,
We're simply passing through,
We've found a higher ground
Walking close to You.
A host of angels surround,
Our hearts rejoice and sing,
Such rich treasures abound,
As to Thy cross we cling;
So, take all we are, all we have,
And all we hope to be...
Use us, Dear Lord, each day we live
To bring glory and honor to Thee.

"That thy way may be known upon earth,
thy saving health among all nations."
(Ps. 67:2)

211

A WONDERFUL CHOIR

The message of a choir singing out
In joyful worship and praise,
Is a glorious anchor for our souls
In the stormy, turbulent days.
God's precious truths shared in song
Reach deep within the soul,
Stirring the heart to follow Christ
More closely in the fold.
Thank God for A Wonderful Choir
That lifts its voice in praise...
Singing the message that keeps us strong
Through all life's stormy days.

"I will offer in his tabernacle sacrifices of joy;
I will sing, yea, I will sing praises unto the Lord."
(Ps. 27:6)

212

THE LIGHTHOUSE

Lord Jesus, You're The Lighthouse
As we sail life's troubled sea...
The Beacon of hope and mercy
That saves and sets us free.
As a sailor seeks a tower
In the dark stormy night,
Our hearts cry out for Thee, Lord –
Our refuge and our Light.
Shine upon the rocks and reefs
Of sins destroying force,
That we might navigate safely
And always stay on course.
Thy wondrous Holy Light
Enables us to see
As we steer toward Glory Land
To live eternally.
Thank You for being The Lighthouse –
Exposing danger around,
As we sail with Thee on the sea of life...
Set free and homeward bound.

"Then spake Jesus... I am the light of the world:
he that followeth me shall not walk in darkness,
but shall have the light of life."
(John 8:12)

GO YE

"Go ye into all the world..."
Take the gospel message to all.
"Ye are the light – the salt of the earth" –
Oh, hear the Master's call.
"The fields are white already to harvest,
But the labourers are few."
May our salt never lose its savour,
But season all we say and do.
Lift high your Light upon a hill,
Let it shine to all around...
That the Father's love would be revealed
And lost souls would be found.
Christ is our Light in this dark world,
Giving spiritual sight to the blind,
Oh, lift Him up for all to see
And let your Light so shine.
We, too, were once in darkness,
But our Saviour set us free,
Now hear the voice of our Loving Lord,
And heed the call – "Go Ye..."

"Go ye into all the world, and preach the gospel to every creature."
"Let your light so shine before men, that they may see
your good works, and glorify your Father which is in heaven."
(Mark 16:15; Matt. 5:16)

THE SIMPLE FAITH OF A CHILD

Jesus said, "Let the little children come unto me
And forbid them not."
They are precious in His sight,
Each and every little tot.
No greater faith in all the world
Than that of a little one
As they come to know Jesus,
God's only begotten Son.
They enter God's kingdom
Freed from the state of sin,
And unless we come as a little child,
We cannot enter in.
It's through simple childlike faith
Grace comes with heaven's bliss;
Such simple believing and trusting
Adults can sometimes miss.
Lord may we be less complex,
More tender, meek and mild;
Help us to always trust You
With The Simple Faith Of A Child.

"Verily I say unto you,
Whosoever shall not receive the kingdom of God
as a little child, he shall not enter therein."
(Mark 10:15)

WHERE THE STILL WATERS FLOW

In the quiet green pastures...
Where the still waters flow,
Our thirsty souls are satisfied
As our Lord we come to know.
There on the righteous paths,
Following close to Him,
Our hearts are safely sheltered,
Though all around is grim.
Even in death's dark shadow
We fear no evil or wrath,
Our Shepherd's there to comfort
With His rod and His staff.
The table spread before us
Gives nourishment we need,
To stand before our enemies
With the strength to succeed.
Oh, what wondrous peace and joy
Our Shepherd doth bestow,
In the quiet green pastures...
Where The Still Waters Flow.

"The Lord is my shepherd; I shall not want.
He maketh me to lie down in green pastures:
He leadeth me beside the still waters.
He restoreth my soul."
(Ps. 1-3)

YOU LIGHT UP OUR LIVES

Lord, You light up our lives...
With Your Glory from on high;
Such joy and peace flood our souls
As we sense Your presence nigh.
You're our Tower on life's sea,
Our Anchor – our security;
And if this world should fall apart,
Your flame will still be in our heart.
Oh, keep us ever close to Thee
Until Thy glorious face we see,
For You and You alone can give
The abundant life that we now live...
As You Light Up Our Lives!

"For thou wilt light my candle:
the Lord my God will enlighten my darkness."
"In him was life; and the life was the light of men."
(Ps. 18:28; John 1:4)

A FAMILY UNITED AS ONE

The church within the church
Is one that cannot fail –
A body of true believers,
Alive and functioning well.
The family of the Living God
Is united in every way,
Living a life of worship and praise,
Serving the Lord each day.
Oh, what blessed fruit bestowed
Upon each believers heart,
When brought into God's family
To be an active part.
Such a precious union in the Father
Who gave His only Son,
To establish His body of believers –
A Family United As One.

"So we, being many, are one body in Christ,
and every one members one of another."
(Rom. 12:5)

Faith Messages V

"O come, let us worship and bow down;
let us kneel before the Lord our maker."
(Psalms 95:6)

D.D.W.

Faith V

In the Garden

In Our Garden Alone
Such Beautiful Roses
The Potter's Hands
Completely Free
A Million Years
Blessings in Time of Trial
We'd Gladly Give
Gloriously Reap
God's Eternal Call
Like an Oak Tree
Bear His Fruit
The Simple Man
A Sure Foundation
He'll Be Your Dad
Time Is Precious
Strength for the Race
Perfect Healing
Redeemed to Serve
Never Give Up in the Valley
A Fountain in the Valley
A Little Portion of Heaven
The Sun Shines So Much
  Brighter
What Manner of Man Is This?
Strength in Christ

A Bright New Life
That Old Rugged Tree
Know Ye Not?
Lord, Thank You
The Song of a Soul Set Free
A Beautiful Creature
Something Out of Nothing
The Prayer of Jabez
It All Goes Back in the Box
You Will Never Be Alone
No Need to Worry
Draw Nigh to God
The One Way Street
My Life Is in His Hands
A Day of Disaster
Resting in Your Hand
God Truly Bless America
What Matters
God Alone
Life Is Worth the Living
So Much More
Walk the Christian Walk
A Holy Living Sanctuary
Little Things

IN OUR GARDEN ALONE

In that private place where we bow our knee
For special time of prayer,
We always sense the presence of God
Each time we enter there;
And oh, what wondrous blessings flow
From His Majestic Throne,
As we hear the voice of our Shepherd...
There In Our Garden Alone.

"When thou prayest, enter into thy closet,
and when thou hast shut thy door,
pray to thy Father which is in secret;
and thy Father which seeth in secret
shall reward thee openly."
(Matt. 6:6)

SUCH BEAUTIFUL ROSES

Fine roses come from the thorns in life –
The trials, heartaches and pain,
As God develops a beauty within us,
Working all for our spiritual gain.
Oh, how we desire that the prickly thorns
Be removed out of our life,
But we'd desire it less if we knew God's best
Comes from that trouble and strife.
Paul prayed his thorn would be removed –
Three times he sought God's hand;
His plea was denied and Paul relied
On the Master's perfect plan.
Oh, how we bargain and beg the Father
To remove our painful thorn,
But we'd desire it less if we knew God's best
And could see the roses form.
As He molds and develops us in His Kingdom,
Such talents and gifts He adorns;
Yet, never has there been a beautiful rosebush
Without the piercing thorns.
Those stakes in our heart we feel unbearable,
And everything in us opposes,
Are the very tools our designer uses...
To develop Such Beautiful Roses.

"For I reckon that the sufferings of this present time are not worthy
to be compared with the glory which shall be revealed in us."
(Rom. 8:18)

THE POTTER'S HANDS

As the Potter's hands are busy
Molding His work of clay,
His vessel becomes more useful
In service to Him each day.
Every trial has its purpose,
Each loss – its infinite gain,
In the life of the Potter's child,
No suffering is in vain.
Tragedy, illness, and sorrow
May shatter our best made plans,
But perfect peace is ours...
Resting in The Potter's Hands.

"O Lord, thou art our father;
we are the clay and thou our potter;
and we all are the work of thy hand."
(Is. 64:8)

COMPLETELY FREE

Oh, do not mourn that I am gone –
I sing a new and glorious song;
I see my Saviour face to face,
Right here where He prepared a place.
Such a reunion at the door,
Greeted by loved ones gone before;
I hear the host of angels sing...
The vict'ry sound shall ever ring.

Oh, do not mourn that I am gone,
For I'm at home where I belong;
No tears or pain on heaven's ground,
God's presence here is all around.
This glorious place beyond the sun
Is where I wait for you dear one,
But until then – joyfully live...
Serve God with all you have to give.

Oh, do not ever mourn for me,
I'm now at home... Completely Free.

"Eye hath not seen, nor ear heard, neither have entered
into the heart of man, the things which God
hath prepared for them that love him."
(I Cor. 2:9)

A MILLION YEARS

If I could have a million years
Of lifetime here on earth,
It still would be too little time
To praise God for new birth;
And if I owned this whole wide world,
What value would it be
Compared to what my Lord has done
To set this sinner free?
How could I pay the debt I owe
The Son of God who came?
He touched my life one glorious day
And I've never been the same.
A new abundant life He gave
To my darkened weary soul;
Somehow He changed my life within
And made my spirit whole.
If I could serve Him day and night
And never close my eyes,
I'd feel I'd just begun to give
To Him who sacrificed;
And if I had A Million Years
Of lifetime here on earth,
It would be far too little time
To praise Him for new birth.

"I will praise thee, O Lord my God, with all my heart:
and I will glorify thy name forevermore."
(Ps. 86:12)

BLESSINGS IN TIME OF TRIAL

When you can't see the blessings
In that trial you're going through,
Turn your eyes upon the Lord
And you'll have a clearer view.
Among the sharp prickly thorns,
Are the roses to be found –
Just focus on the Saviour
And you'll see them all around.
He is the Rose of Sharon,
The bright and morning Star –
Touched with your infirmities,
He's right there where you are.
Just keep your eyes upon Him
Whatever you go through,
He's your friend beyond compare –
The One who died for you.
Though Satan tries to break you
When those trials come your way,
Christ never will forsake you...
He'll bless you every day.

"For he hath said, I will never leave thee, nor forsake thee."
"In a great trial of affliction the abundance of their joy
and their deep poverty abounded unto
the riches of their liberality."
(Heb. 13:5; II Cor. 8:2)

WE'D GLADLY GIVE

Our own lives we'd gladly give
For those we hold so dear
To be delivered from eternal death –
Darkness, torment and fear.
We'd be their savior if we could,
And suffer in their place,
If only they could know the joy
Of God's amazing grace.
He and He alone can free
A lost and weary soul,
Purify a sinful heart
And make our loved ones whole;
But if we could be their savior
And suffer in their place,
We'd do it in a heartbeat
For them to know God's grace.
Oh, how we pray our loved ones
Would come to Christ and live;
For our kinsmen in the flesh...
Our own lives We'd Gladly Give.

"For I could wish that myself were accursed from Christ
for my brethren, my kinsmen according to the flesh."
(Rom. 9:3)

GLORIOUSLY REAP

Adding to our faith virtue –
Purging ourselves from sin,
The richest blessings of all are found
As our hearts are cleansed within;
Adding to virtue knowledge
Of God's precious Holy Word,
Our walk of faith is strengthened,
And with Truth our loins are gird;
Adding to knowledge temperance –
Manifesting the fruit within,
Our witness becomes much sweeter,
Touching the hearts of men;
Adding to temperance patience,
More fruit in us revealed
As we learn to live peaceably,
And to our Saviour yield;
Adding to patience godliness –
Living a righteous life,
Fierce storms may rage all about,
We're safe in the midst of strife;

Adding to godliness brotherly kindness,
And to brotherly kindness charity,
We shall neither be barren or unfruitful,
But Gloriously Reap eternally.

"Giving all diligence, add to your faith virtue;
and to virtue knowledge;
And to knowledge temperance;
and to temperance godliness;
And to godliness, brotherly kindness;
and to brotherly kindness charity,
For if these things be in you, and abound,
they make you that ye shall
neither be barren nor unfruitful in the knowledge
of our Lord Jesus Christ."
"For so an entrance shall be ministered
unto you abundantly into the everlasting kingdom
of our Lord and Saviour Jesus Christ."
(II Pet. 1:5-8, 11)

GOD'S ETERNAL CALL

Take the glitter and the glamour
And all it's temporal pleasure,
In my Lord I've found a storehouse
Of everlasting treasure.
This world's trinkets and romance
Hold no attraction for me,
They can't compare with what I have
Since my Lord hath set me free.
I want no part of the tempter's charms,
There's just simply no appeal,
In my precious Lord I've found
Eternal joy that's really real.
I'm looking for His soon return –
It could be any day,
And when He comes I want to be
Walking the narrow way.
Oh, how I long to see Him
Clearly face to face,
And thank Him for abundant life
And His amazing grace.

Take Satan's worldly playhouse –
I want no part at all,
For I'm basking in the sunlight
Of God's Eternal Call.

"Love not the world, neither the things that are in the world.
If any man love the world, the love of the Father is not in him.
For all that is in the world, the lust of the flesh, and the lust of the
eyes, and the pride of life, is not of the Father, but is of the world.
And the world passeth away, and the lust thereof:
but he that doeth the will of God abideth for ever."
(I John 2:15-17)

LIKE AN OAK TREE

I'd like to be like an Oak Tree
As God reveals His Truth to me,
For an Oak has great capacity
For strength in the midst of adversity –
Sturdiness in the roughest breeze,
Standing firm among weaker trees;
Oh, if I could just be like an Oak Tree,
Unmoved when rough winds beat upon me,
Perhaps I could help the weaker I see,
And somehow my life just might be
A witness to Truth that sets man free.
Father, may my roots grow deep in Thee
As more of Thy precious Word I see,
That I may be... Like An Oak Tree.

"... rooted and built up in him and stablished in the faith..."
"Be ye steadfast, unmovable, always abounding
in the work of the Lord,
Forasmuch as ye know that your
labor is not in vain in the Lord."
(Col. 2:7; I Cor. 15:58)

BEAR HIS FRUIT

Our Heavenly Father's the husbandman,
Our Lord Jesus Christ the Vine;
We're the branches abiding in Him,
Bearing fruit for all mankind.
The branch can do nothing without the Vine,
For no life abides within;
But through the Word it's made alive
As God purges from all sin.
Oh, may we always bear that fruit so sweet
Of our precious Lord who came,
Lest we be a branch withering away,
Having taken His name in vain.
Continuing in love, keeping His word,
Our hearts are purified,
And as we bear the fruit of His Spirit,
Our Father is glorified.
Oh, what joy flows from the Vine
As we walk God's holy way;
Loving one another as He loved us,
We Bear His Fruit each day.

Jesus said: "I am the vine, ye are the branches:
He that abideth in me, and I in him, the same bringeth forth
much fruit: for without me ye can do nothing."
"Herein is my Father glorified, that ye bear much fruit;
so shall ye be my disciples."
(John 15:5, 8)

THE SIMPLE MAN

Oh, let me walk with the simple man,
I want no fortune or fame,
No power, prestige or honor,
For I know from whence I came.
Bestow no glory upon me, my friend,
No praise or adoration,
For not one thing could I ever do
To earn such salutation;
But there's One who came so long ago
To bear our sin and shame –
He and He alone is worthy
Of such honor to His Name.
My hands I raise in joyful praise
Singing Glory to my King,
And my knees I bow in worship
As to His cross I cling.
Should e'er I attain some great work
I'd count it all but loss...
Just let me walk with the simple man
And remain at the foot of the cross.

"But what things were gain to me, those I counted loss for Christ."
"I count all things but loss for the excellency
of the knowledge of Christ Jesus my Lord."
(Phil. 3:7-8)

A SURE FOUNDATION

We're building in the Kingdom
Of our Holy Righteous God...
A house that's strong and sturdy,
Founded not on earthly sod.
The Master Builder guides us
As He gives to us His plans,
And as we closely follow,
He'll use our feeble hands.
Let us take heed how we build,
Our foundation is the best;
It shall ever hold secure
Through each fiery trial and test.
When those turbulent winds blow
And forceful rains beat down,
Resting on this foundation...
Our house is safe and sound;
For it's not built upon the sand
Or on any temporal sod,
But on the solid Rock of Ages –
The Son of The Living God.

"For other foundation can no man lay than that is laid,
which is Jesus Christ."
"And the rain descended, and the floods came,
and the winds blew, and beat upon that house;
and it fell not: for it was founded upon a rock."
(I Cor. 3:11; Matt. 7:25)

HE'LL BE YOUR DAD

If you have a wonderful Dad
Who loves and cares for you,
What a blessing from the Lord!
Honor Him in all you do.
And when Dad is unavailable,
There's One who will provide,
He'll always take good care of you,
For He's right there by your side.
He's a Father to the fathers,
And to the fatherless;
A Husband to the widows,
And His family's always blessed.
He is wealthy in every way –
He owns the cattle and the hills,
Yet, He's never too busy for you,
And somehow that void He fills.
So never feel hurt little one
If your earthly father's away,
Your Heavenly Father's with you
To love and keep you every day.
As you pray and look to Him,
Never you fear little lad,
He'll provide all you ever need –
He'll even be your Dad.

And don't you be lonely little girl,
Or let your heart be sad,
The One who made this whole wide world
Loves you, and He'll Be Your Dad.

"Honor thy father and thy mother as
the Lord thy God hath commanded thee."
"A father of the fatherless, and a judge of
the widows, is God in his holy habitation."
"He relieveth the fatherless and widow."
(Deut. 5:16; Ps. 68:5; Ps. 146:9)

TIME IS PRECIOUS

Is there something you'd like to change –
Something you feel you should do?
Oh, do not hesitate my friend,
For the days are short and few.
Time is just so very precious –
Every moment of the day;
More valuable than fine jewels,
Do not squander it away.
Nothing's ever done yesterday,
And tomorrow has yet to come,
It is only in the today
That anything ever is done.
As you buy and sell, work and play,
Just make sure the Lord is in it,
For there's never a guarantee
Of another single minute.
Time's a gift to be used on earth,
In preparation for eternity,
And what we do within its span,
Determines our soul's destiny.
Be very sure you know the Lord,
And on Him completely rely…
Obey His word, love and serve Him,
Before Time passes you by.

"Behold, now is the accepted time; behold, now is the day of salvation."
"Seek ye the Lord while he may be found, call ye upon him while he is nea
"See then that ye walk circumspectly, not as fools, but as wise,
redeeming the time for the days are evil."
(II Cor. 6:2; Is. 55:6; Eph. 5:15-16)

STRENGTH FOR THE RACE

God gives us the strength to run life's race,
And the stamina needed to keep the pace;
He uses the circumstances we go through
To condition us for what He calls us to do.
He strengthens our hearts, souls and minds,
And lifts sin's weight that so easily binds,
That we might run with honor and grace
Through those difficult obstacles we face.
As we run, He is with us along the way,
Refreshing, and supplying our need each day;
If we focus on Him and never look back,
We'll always be running on the right track.
Across the line – is a crown to be received,
For all we've accomplished and achieved;
We'll accept it gladly when the race is complete,
To lay at our wonderful Trainer's feet.
Praise God! With Christ as our Coach Divine,
We don't have to wait for the finish line...
Hallelujah! The victory already is won,
We can rejoice right now as the race is run.
Father, we thank Thee for Thy saving grace
That imparts to us – Strength for the Race.

"The Lord will give strength unto his people."
"Let us run with patience the race that is set before us,
Looking unto Jesus the author and finisher of our faith."
(Ps. 29:11; Heb. 12:1-2)

239

PERFECT HEALING

Greater than any physical problems
That plague our lives with pain,
Are the spiritual problems apart from Christ
With self on the throne to reign.
Physical ailments can affect our lives
Only to a certain degree,
But spiritual death affects our souls
Through time and eternity.
Oh, do not turn away from Christ,
Hear His sovereign call,
And receive new spiritual life in Him...
The most Perfect Healing of all.

"He sent his word, and healed them,
and delivered them from their destructions."
"The Word was made flesh, and dwelt among us."
(Ps. 107:20; John 1:14)

REDEEMED TO SERVE

Redeemed by the precious blood of the Lamb,
Forgiven and cleansed within,
Showers of blessings fall all around
Since He washed away our sin.
God forbid we keep such blessings
Merely for ourselves alone,
We have been redeemed to glorify God
And make His message known;
Redeemed to serve in His Kingdom
And proclaim His Truth throughout,
To a world searching and thirsting,
Lost in unbelief and doubt.
Our lives were purchased at Calvary,
The ultimate price was paid...
Christ loved us more than life itself
And His own He gladly gave.
Redeemed and so happy in Jesus,
Yet, so burdened for the lost;
Oh, God, take our lives and use us
Regardless of the cost.

"Christ hath redeemed us from the curse of the law..."
"Then said Jesus to them... as my Father hath
sent me, even so send I you."
(Gal. 3:13; John 20:21)

NEVER GIVE UP IN THE VALLEY

Never give up in the valley,
For it's a sacred place to be;
Allow God to mold and shape you
Into the vessel He'd have you be.
Trust Him to work within your soul
When tried by the flames of fire,
He'll bring you forth, pure as gold,
To a ground that's so much higher.
Many turn back in valley times,
Fearing the trouble and strife,
Never to reach that higher plain
Of blessings and service in life;
But as you focus on the Saviour,
The deep pathway's not so grim;
He will light the darkest night,
As you keep your eyes on Him.
Just rest in His sovereign hands
Whatever you're going through,
And Never Give Up in the Valley...
Let God develop you.

"... that the trial of your faith, being much more precious
than of gold that perisheth, though it be tried with fire,
might be found unto praise and honour
and glory at the appearing of Jesus Christ."
(I Peter 1:7)

A FOUNTAIN IN THE VALLEY

In the midst of the deepest valley,
There's a Fountain springing up
With the Water of Life that satisfies,
And fills the empty cup.
This Fountain, so freely flowing,
Refreshes the thirsty soul,
And all who come for healing
Are cleansed within, and made whole.
Whosoever drinks of this Water
Shall never thirst again;
And no matter how rough the valley,
Enduring strength is within.
It's the Fountain of everlasting life,
And it never shall run dry;
All who partake shall live forever,
And enjoy an endless supply.
Oh, come and drink from this Water,
Come and be made whole...
There's A Fountain in the Valley
To satisfy your soul.

Jesus said: "If any man thirst, let him come unto me, and drink.
He that believeth on me, as the scripture hath said,
out of his belly shall flow rivers of living water."
(John 7:37-38)

A LITTLE PORTION OF HEAVEN

If there were no other reason to go to church
But to obey God's command,
I'd want to be there every service
And be part of His great plan.
I'd want to work and serve the Master,
Or just worship at His feet;
Where His people are gathered together
Is always a sweet retreat.
I would go because I love Him so
And just couldn't stay away,
And because I love His family
And want to join with them to pray.
I love hearing His word proclaimed –
Learning His will and way,
The knowledge of my precious Lord
Gives me strength for the day.
I love to hear the glorious choir
As the joyful voices are raised,
And I love joining in to sing
Songs of victory and praise;
But if there were no other reason
But to obey God's command,
I'd want to be there every service
For that special touch of His hand.
What a great privilege is ours
As we go to God's house of prayer;
We find each time we meet,
His Holy Spirit's there.
When we come to know our Saviour
In the spiritual new birth,
Church is A Little Portion of Heaven
Granted to us on earth.

"Not forsaking the assembling of ourselves together, as the
manner of some is; but exhorting one another: and so much
the more, as ye see the day approaching."
(Heb. 10:25)

THE SUN SHINES SO MUCH BRIGHTER

The sun shines so much brighter
Since my Lord I came to know;
Those heavy burdens lifted...
The garden takes on a glow.
Never had I ever seen
Such a glory in a flower,
Till my weary soul was saved
By God's mercy, grace and power.
The moon now shines to praise Him,
As I've never seen before,
And the shining stars above
Now are sparkling even more.
As I look up toward heaven,
And on this earth all around,
I can only stand in awe
Of such beauty to be found.
What a wondrous change takes place
As our eyes are opened to view
The creation of our God
Through a heart made clean and new.
A portion of His kingdom
Lights this earth with heaven's glow...
The Sun Shines So Much Brighter
Since my Lord I came to know.

"Praise ye him, sun and moon: praise him, all ye stars of light."
"The light of the moon shall be as the light of the sun, and the light
of the sun shall be sevenfold... in the day that the Lord bindeth up the
breach of his people, and healeth the stroke of their wound."
(Ps. 148:3; Isa. 30:26)

WHAT MANNER OF MAN IS THIS?

"What manner of man is this
That even the wind and sea obey...?"
Every step on earth He took
Miracles happened in that day.
He walked upon the water,
And turned water into wine;
He unstopped the ears of the deaf,
And opened the eyes of the blind;
He healed the sick, raised the dead,
He touched and healed the lame;
He fed a crowd with a little lunch,
And forgave all who humbly came;
He spoke and the storm was still,
Even the sea obeyed His will;
He claimed to be God's own Son,
And willingly died on the cross;
His precious blood, shed for man,
Was a ransom for the lost.
He arose just as He said,
And walked and talked among men,
Then ascended into heaven...
The price was paid for sin.
This man who walked among us
Gives life and eternal bliss
To all who bow before Him...
"What Manner of Man is This...?"

"Thou art the Christ, the Son of the living God."
(Matt. 16:16)

246

STRENGTH IN CHRIST

So often we limit ourselves,
Feeling inadequate and shy;
Afraid we cannot measure up,
We give up before we try...
But our strength comes from above
For the task God calls us to,
And His grace is all sufficient
For whatever we go through.
Where His Holy Spirit leads,
He'll abundantly provide;
He will meet our every need,
For He's right there by our side.
Our Lord is strong and mighty
And we're so weak and frail,
But empowered by His Spirit
We shall evermore prevail.
As our eyes are stayed on Him,
Closely following His lead,
We find our Strength in Christ...
And He's all we'll ever need!

"I can do all things through Christ
which stengtheneth me."
(Phil. 4:13)

A BRIGHT NEW LIFE

When despair fills your weary soul
And there's just no way to cope;
When you think your life is over
And you see no ray of hope...
A light shines forth in the darkness
That will brighten your pathway...
It will bring down heaven's glory
And a brand new, happy day.
It's the Light of our Lord Jesus,
Precious Saviour, God and King;
His grace is free to all who bow
At the cross... their sins to bring.
This wonderful grace and mercy
Will free your spirit to sing...
Praises to God in the highest,
As you worship your great King.
The valleys won't seem so deep,
For you'll never walk alone;
You'll always have a perfect peace
And joy like you've never known.
Oh, friend, when you come to the end,
A new day awaits your soul...
The Saviour's there to pardon you,
He will cleanse and make you whole.
Just come to the cross of Calvary
And lay it all down at His feet...
You'll find amazing grace in Christ,
And A Bright New Life so sweet.

Jesus said: "I have come that they might have life,
and that they might have it more abundantly."
"In him was life; and the life was the light of men."
(John 10:10; John 1:4)

THAT OLD RUGGED TREE

Had it not been for that rugged tree,
There on a hill called Calvary,
Where Your precious blood was shed for me,
I'd still be blind and could not see;
I'd be bound by sin's captivity,
Not knowing life abundantly,
I'd have no peace or joy in Thee...
Thank You, Lord, for That Old Rugged Tree!

Had You not willingly died for me,
I would be lost eternally,
No where to turn, no where to flee,
No one to hear my desperate plea;
My sinful soul would never be free,
I would not know Your love for me,
Had it not been for Calvary...
Thank You, Lord, for That Old Rugged Tree!

"And when they came to the place called Calvary,
there they crucified him."
"The blood of Jesus Christ his Son
cleanseth us from all sin."
(Luke 23:33; I John 1:7)

KNOW YE NOT?

Know ye not He came to save your soul,
To willingly die on a tree?
Know ye not His blood can make you whole,
That it avails for you and me?
Know ye not He came forth from the tomb,
Hallelujah!... our Risen King?
Know ye not Christ Jesus lives today
To forgive and to make you clean?

Know ye not ye are God's own temple
When His presence in you abides?
Know ye not there's grace and glory
Where His Holy Spirit resides?
Know ye not He is coming again
To receive His forgiven bride?
Know ye not the time is, Oh, so close?...
Be sure the Lord you've not denied.

"Christ Jesus came into the world to save sinners."
"Know ye not that ye are the temple of God,
and that the Spirit of Goddwelleth in you?
If any man defile the temple of God, him shall God destroy;
for the temple of God is holy, which temple ye are."
(I Tim. 1:15; I Cor. 3:16-17)

LORD, THANK YOU

Lord, You're my all, my everything;
My Master, Saviour, God and King;
You are my sunshine and my rain,
Forevermore I'll praise Your Name...
Lord, thank You for saving me.

You are the water that I need,
The bread of life my soul to feed;
You are my strength from day to day,
My solid rock, my hope, my stay...
Lord, thank You for keeping me.

Your Glory shines into my heart;
It reaches each and every part;
The beams of joyful Holy Light
Brighten the darkest dreary night...
Lord, thank You for illumining me.

Your guiding hand shows me the way
As I open Your word and pray;
Your Holy Spirit is so near,
Your still small voice so very clear...
Lord, thank You for leading me.

Your loving arms are open wide
As I come to you to confide;
My broken heart You take and mend;
You are my very dearest Friend...
Lord, Thank You for loving me.

"Bless the Lord, O my soul, and forget not all his benefits"
"Let us come before his presence with thanksgiving."
(Ps. 103:1-2; Ps. 95:2)

THE SONG OF A SOUL SET FREE

We have a new and glorious song,
One of joyful praise and love,
To sing through all eternity,
Right here and in heaven above.
It's the song of a soul set free,
A sheep brought into the fold;
A wondrous melody rings out
Since, by grace, God made us whole.
Delivered from sin and darkness
To sing with the saints on high,
Now together in heavenly places,
Since our Lord hath drawn us nigh.
Singing the song of victory,
United we lift our voice,
Our hearts now raised to sing His praise,
All heaven's angels rejoice.
It's the song of a soul set free,
Free to worship and obey,
Free to love our God supremely,
Free to serve Him every day.
This glorious song that we now sing,
We shall sing forevermore;
It's The Song of a Soul Set Free...
Free to enter heaven's door.

"And he hath put a new song in my mouth, even praise unto our God:
many shall see it, and fear, and shall trust in the Lord."
(Ps. 40:3)

A BEAUTIFUL CREATURE

As a caterpillar sheds its skin...
And changes into a butterfly,
A repentant soul sheds its sin...
And to its old tattered self doth die.
In the pupal stage it's warmed,
According to God's great plan;
There a new being is formed,
Created by His own hand.
Hallelujah! One glorious day
The miracle birth takes place...
In God's own time, and in His way,
A soul is freed by grace.
Oh, what a change is wrought...
Such a wretched worm – a lowly sight,
Who would have ever thought
A Beautiful Creature would take flight?

"Therefore if any man be in Christ, he is a new creature:
old things have passed away; behold,
all things are become new."
(II Cor. 5:17)

SOMETHING OUT OF NOTHING

God made something out of nothing
When this world His hands did form;
He simply spoke and there was light –
A bright sun, the earth to warm.
God made something out of nothing
When He hung the moon in space;
Then He took mere dust from the ground
And He made the human race.

God still makes something from nothing,
As His Spirit moves on earth,
Calling the lost to the Saviour,
He imparts new spiritual birth.
He makes something out of nothing
When He hears the humble cry...
He gives water in the desert
As a thirsty soul draws nigh.

God made something out of nothing
When He saved this soul of mine;
He made something out of nothing
When He gave new life divine.
God made something out of nothing
When He heard my desperate plea...
He made Something Out of Nothing
When He set this sinner free.

"The first man is of the earth, earthy:
the second man is the Lord from heaven."
"For if a man think himself to be something,
when he is nothing, he deceiveth himself."
"We are his workmanship, created in Christ Jesus unto good works."
(I Cor. 15:47; Gal. 6:3; Eph. 2:10)

THE PRAYER OF JABEZ

Jabez prayed: "Oh Lord, bless me indeed."
God answered... and more than met his need.
He prayed the Lord would enlarge his field,
And God's Spirit... a vision revealed.
He asked for the Lord's almighty hand,
And God was with him... working His plan.
He asked to be kept from evil's harm,
And God shielded... with His mighty arm.
By faith, Jabez knew his God was there,
And so God granted... his earnest prayer.
Such a little portion of God's Word,
Yet, such a powerful message is heard.
Oh, that our Lord would bless us indeed,
Enlarge our vision for those in need,
And be with us, His hand to reveal,
As we bear witness that He is real.
He'll keep us from sin, evil and harm,
As we depend on His loving arm.
The God of Jabez is our God too...
He'll answer that prayer for me and you.

"Oh that thou wouldest bless me indeed, and enlarge my coast,
and that thine hand might be with me, and that thou wouldest
keep me from evil, that it may not grieve me!
And God granted him that which he requested."
(I Ch. 4:10)

255

IT ALL GOES BACK IN THE BOX

Someone has said: "Life is like a Monopoly game"
And this message is so true;
All the buildings, houses, land, and cash,
Go back in the box when through.
Life in Christ our Lord, and deeds in Him,
No human can take away,
But the things acquired while on this earth
Go back in the box one day.
An extended hand to one in need
Brings blessings from the Lord;
A cup of water given in His Name
Shall reap eternal reward.
Reaching out to a soul whose bound...
We lay up treasures in heaven,
And enjoy the benefits here and now
As God's true riches are given.
But the clothes, the cars, the stocks and bonds,
The jewelry – the diamond rocks,
Even the body... when the game ends...
It All Goes Back in the Box.

"The things which are seen are temporal;
but the things which are not seen are eternal."
"Labour not for the meat which perisheth,
but for that meat which endureth unto everlasting life."
"Lay not up for yourselves treasures upon earth...
But lay up for yourselves treasures in heaven...
For where your treasure is, there will your heart be also."
(II Cor. 4:18; John 6:27; Matt. 6:19-21)

YOU WILL NEVER BE ALONE

When you are feeling all alone
Down-hearted, sad and blue,
And you think that there's just no one
Who really cares for you,
Just look above and you will see
A Friend so near and dear;
His tender love and gentle care
Is offered you right here.
Christ gave His very life for you...
No greater love than this;
No need to wait for heaven's gate
To know true joy and bliss;
Just surrender your all to Him,
You'll be so richly blessed;
He'll be your Lord and dearest Friend
And give to you His best.
When you are down, He'll lift you up,
He'll warm a heart grown cold;
His heavenly manna from above
Will satisfy your soul.
In Him you'll find a peace and joy
Like you have never known,
He'll walk beside you evermore...
You Will Never Be Alone.

"I will never leave thee, nor forsake thee."
(Heb. 13:5)

NO NEED TO WORRY

Some days we walk a lonely road
And carry such a heavy load,
'Neath the sin of worry and fret.
Our strength is just too weak to bear
The heavy burden we find there...
We meet with anguish and regret.

But when we look above and pray,
We hear our loving Shepherd say:
"Rely on Me in all you do.
And when you do not understand,
Just rest completely in My hand...
You can trust Me to lead you through."

When we obey that voice we hear,
The Holy Spirit's... Oh, so near...
That burden's gone we had before;
And as we walk the road with Him,
He lights our way when all is grim...
No Need to Worry Anymore.

"Trust in the Lord, and do good."
"Cast thy burden upon the Lord,
and he shall sustain thee."
(Ps. 37:3; 55:22)

DRAW NIGH TO GOD

When death comes nigh our dwelling
Everything stops – time stands still.
We're pliable in God's hands
As we submit to His will.
Oh, if we'd just draw that close
In the day of prosperity...
Be still, listen, seek His will,
Prepare for eternity...
Our God would bless us indeed;
His Spirit would be poured out,
Reaching far beyond ourselves,
Impacting this world throughout...
If we'd just Draw Nigh to God.

"Draw nigh to God and He will draw nigh to you."
(James 4:8)

THE ONE WAY STREET

On the broad path of destruction,
Souls in bondage remain,
Though the map of life, the Bible,
Points to a higher plain.
Many have made a profession,
Yet never really heard
The true message of salvation
From God's own written word.

How could one walk the lowly path,
Still blind and deaf and dumb?
The gospel news is all around...
The King of Glory hath come;
Having ears to hear, they hear not
Of life's secure highway,
And continue down sin's dark road
To face the Judgment Day.

The narrow path is paved with love,
Our Saviour paid the cost,
His wondrous Light shines all around...
No fear of getting lost.
It's The One Way Street to Glory,
God's Spirit within to guide,
Walking the joyful path of life...
On the Hallelujah side.

"Narrow is the way, which leadeth unto life, and few there be that find it."
"Thou wilt shew me the path of life: in thy presence is fullness of joy;
at thy right hand are pleasures for evermore."
(Matt. 7:14; Ps. 16:11)

MY LIFE IS IN HIS HANDS

I know not what tomorrow may bring...
Just what the future holds,
But I know I can rejoice and sing
No matter what unfolds.
The God of all the earth is near...
I'm resting in His hands;
Not one thing touches my life here
That's not within His plans.
He cares about the things I do...
His watchful eye sees all;
In troubled times, He sees me through,
Holding me lest I fall.
I rest secure in stormy days
When I can't see ahead,
Trusting in Him, I sing His praise,
And by His hand I'm led.
In peaceful times, when the storm's o'er,
There in His arms I stay,
For sin entices me no more
Walking the King's highway.
My heart now bears His mark and seal,
According to His plans,
My God is here, and He is real...
My Life is in His Hands.

Jesus said: "No man is able to pluck them out of my Father's hand."
(John 10:29)

A DAY OF DISASTER
(September 11, 2001)

The horrific events of this dark day
Compel our hearts to seek God and pray...
Turning to the Master.
As evil forces strike our great land,
Lives are lost at the enemy's hand...
A day of disaster.
Godly men simply can't comprehend
Twisted minds that concoct such a sin...
So despicably vile.
Make no mistake, hearts loving and meek,
Empowered by God, are never weak...
Though Satan may beguile.
Let us move forward in grace and power
To meet the challenge of this dark hour...
Regardless of the cost.
Oh, God, we bow before Thee in prayer –
Undergird in this burden we bear...
Lest our freedoms be lost.

As we humbly seek Thy Holy Face,
Grant forgiveness, wisdom, strength and grace...
Found in Christ our Master.
Faced with Thy Spirit's Mighty Power,
The enemy is doomed this very hour...
A Day of Disaster!

"If thou shalt hearken diligently unto the voice of
the Lord thy God, to observe and to do all his commandments...
the Lord thy God will set thee on high
above all nations of the earth."
"The Lord shall cause thine enemies that rise up
against thee to be smitten before thy face."
(Deut. 28:1, 7)

RESTING IN YOUR HAND

Lord, take us, shape us, mold us, and make us,
Help us to understand,
Though Satan's forces attempt to break us...
You hold us in Your hand.

No evil force on earth can thwart Your plan,
Though fiery darts assail,
Resting securely in Your sovereign hand...
We'll evermore prevail.

And should one day the outer man perish,
At the enemy's hand,
In Glory we shall live and reign with You...
According to Your plan.

So, take us, shape us, mold us, and make us,
Help us to understand,
The victory is ours forevermore...
Resting in Your Hand.

"Whether we live therefore, or die, we are the Lord's."
"There remaineth therefore a rest to the people of God."
(Rom. 14:8; Heb. 4:9)

GOD TRULY BLESS AMERICA

Oh, God, truly bless America
As our wayward hearts confess;
Impart Thy goodness, peace and joy,
Turn us back to righteousness.
Grant Forgiveness – as we bow to Thee,
Grace – as we kneel;
Wisdom – as we turn to Thee,
Strength – as we yield.
Bless our land with moral fiber –
Lift us from degradation;
Bless us with freedom's Holy Light –
Oh, how we need salvation.
Grant Purity – as we worship Thee,
Comfort – as we lean on Thee,
Courage – as we trust in Thee,
Victory – as we cling to Thee.
May we, one nation under Thee,
Move in Thy Spirit's power,
And in the Name of Christ our Lord,
Meet the challenge of this hour.
Oh, God, truly bless America,
Bless our great land indeed;
Give liberty that we might be
A beacon to those in need...
God Truly Bless America!

"Righteousness exalteth a nation; but sin is a reproach to any people."
"If my people, which are called by my name, shall humble themselves,
and pray, and seek my face, and turn from their wicked ways; then will
I hear from heaven, and will forgive their sin, and will heal their land."
"Humble yourselves therefore under the mighty hand of God,
that he may exalt you in due time:"
(Prov. 14:34; II Ch. 7:14; I Pet. 5:6)

WHAT MATTERS

What matters is not how deep the valley,
Nor how dark the lonely night,
But the closeness of our loving Shepherd,
Our Comforter – our guiding Light.

He who holds our hand when we need a friend,
And carries His helpless sheep,
Lights our path with His Glorious Presence,
Our hearts and souls to keep.

What matters is not how big the problem,
Nor those obstacles we face,
But the strength and power of our Great God,
And His sustaining grace.

"The Lord is my Shepherd; I shall not want."
"Great is our Lord, and of great power."
"Cast thy burden upon the Lord,
and he shall sustain thee."
(Ps. 23:1; 147:5; 55:22)

GOD ALONE

God alone knows what the future holds,
He alone knows the fate of men's souls,
Only His hand sovereignly controls...
Trust In Him and Him alone.

God alone knows what's around the bend,
He alone knows the hearts of all men,
Only He knows what is best to send...
Worship before His Throne.

God alone knows what each day will bring,
To our Majestic Lord let us cling,
And with rejoicing hearts ever sing...
Praise to God and God Alone.

"He ruleth by his power for ever; his eyes behold the nations."
The Lord knoweth the days of the upright;
and their inheritance shall be for ever."
"Praise ye the Lord. O give thanks
unto the Lord for he is good."
(Ps. 66:7; 37:18; 106:1)

LIFE IS WORTH THE LIVING

Life is worth the living
When all is sunny and bright,
And it's worth the living
In the darkest stormy night;
Life is worth the living
When high on the mountain peak,
And it's worth the living
When down in the valley deep.

Life is worth the living...
Because our Saviour is near,
It is worth the living
As He blesses us right here;
Life is worth the living,
His loving presence makes it so,
Yes, it's worth the living...
When our Lord we come to know.

"The Lord is my strength and song, and is become my salvation."
"I shall not die, but live, and declare the works of the Lord."
"The Lord is the strength of my life."
(Ps. 118:14, 17; 27:1)

SO MUCH MORE

If we love our children who go astray,
The relative who's unkind,
The souls we meet along life's way
Whose spiritual eyes are blind,
If we being human can love them so,
How much more does our Lord God
Love all creatures here below?
That question was settled long ago
On the Cross of Calvary,
Where the precious blood of the Lamb
Was shed for you and me.
To this whole world our God revealed
The answer from shore to shore...
His great love is beyond compare –
He loves us So Much More!

"If ye then, being evil, know how to give
good gifts unto your children:
How much more shall your heavenly Father
give the Holy Spirit to them that ask him?"
"Greater love hath no man than this,
that a man lay down his life for his friends."
(Luke 11:13; John 15:13)

WALK THE CHRISTIAN WALK

So many walk contrary
To the teachings of God's Word,
Yet they've made a profession
And so often have heard.
God hates the hypocrisy
Throughout the world today-
Those who profess, but don't possess,
Eat, drink and rise to play;
But all who truly repent
Shall genuinely come to know
The God of grace and glory
Who loves His creatures below.
To know Him is to love Him,
Let us not just talk the talk;
If we possess let us profess...
And Walk The Christian Walk.

"He that saith he abideth in him ought himself
also so to walk, even as he walked."
"If we live in the Spirit, let us also walk in the spirit."
"As ye have therefore received Christ Jesus
the Lord, so walk ye in him:"
(I John 2:6; Gal. 5:25; Col. 2:6)

A HOLY LIVING SANCTUARY

Our bodies are the temple of God,
To be kept pure and clean –
A Holy Living Sanctuary
Where God's great Truth is seen.
His Holy Spirit abides within,
Abundant life to bring...
We're set apart for sacred service
As we worship our King.
Only by the blood of Christ our Lord
Can we be purified,
And only walking close with Him
Are our hearts sanctified.
Lord, keep us close and our temple clean,
Enable us to be
A Holy Living Sanctuary...
As we humbly serve Thee.

"Know ye not that ye are the temple of God,
And that the Spirit of God dwelleth in you?"
If any man defile the temple of God, him shall God destroy;
For the temple of God is holy, which temple ye are."
(I Cor. 3:16-17)

LITTLE THINGS

A little drop of rain that falls,
A little ray of sun,
A little flower that soon grows,
And we've only just begun...
The little things we see in life
Can mean the very most,
Much more than big accomplishments
Of which we often boast.
A little leaf breaks loose and falls
In such a gentle way;
A little smile can warm the heart
And brighten up our day.
A little garden means so much,
That little seed just needs God's touch;
A little faith, a little prayer...
What a big God we meet there!

"O Lord God, thou hast begun to shew thy servant thy greatness,
and thy mighty hand: for what God is there in heaven
or in earth, that can do according to thy works
and according to thy might?"
(Deut. 3:24)

Faith Messages VI

"If ye walk in my statutes,
and keep my commandments and do them..."
"I will give peace in the land, and ye shall lie down,
and none shall make you afraid."
(Leviticus 26:3, 6)

Faith VI

Let There Be Peace

Perfect Peace
He's Still Faithful
A Glorious Hope
He's Coming Very Soon
Peace with Thee
Those Great Trials
Thank You, Lord
When You Can't Understand
The Victory's Ours
The King's Holy Highway
Rather Than
The Greatest Blessings
The Greatest Miracle
Peace on Earth
The Weight of Sin
Precious Name
Precious Promises
Translated Into His Kingdom
The Master's Vineyard
God Is There for You
God, Give Us Christians!
The Test of Christianity
Evidence of Things Not Seen
Just Let Me Live for Thee
The Anchor of My Soul

Come to Christ Today
Lest I Fall Away
The Light Within
When God Leads, He Will
    Provide
Touched with Our Infirmities
Touched by the Master's
    Hand
Take My Hand, Lord
Until Then
Surrender All
While There's Still Time
No Other Friend Like Jesus
Do We Love Him?
A Voice in the Wilderness
If I'd Never Seen
Fishers of Men
I Believe
I Am Not Ashamed
Not By Bread Alone
A Place of Beginning Again
The Only Way
As the Moon Rises
Lift Up Your Eyes
True Peace

PERFECT PEACE

In the midst of troubled waters,
On the sea of war and strife,
A Beacon of Light shines brightly...
Giving Peace and eternal Life.

No matter how rough the waters,
Though the fury may never cease,
Our Anchor holds securely...
Christ is our Perfect Peace.

"Thou wilt keep him in perfect peace,
whose mind is stayed on thee."
"For He is our peace."
(Isa. 26:3; Eph. 2:14)

HE'S STILL FAITHFUL

Christ – the solid Rock, the Tower of refuge,
The Haven of restful calm,
Still reaches out in the worst of times...
With a soothing, healing balm.
He's the peace that passes understanding
That this world cannot give;
The joy unspeakable and full of glory...
The abundant life we live.
He's the undergirding Strength in fiery trials,
Giving grace to endure;
The Anchor planted deep within our souls...
Holding safe and secure.
He is still our loving Shepherd and Friend
When our dreams fall apart;
And He's Still Faithful to all who heed His call...
Surrendering their heart.

"I have been young, and now am old;
yet have I not seen the righteous
forsaken, nor his seed begging bread."
"The Lord is faithful, who shall establish you,
and keep you from evil."
(Ps. 37:25; II Thes. 3:3)

A GLORIOUS HOPE

In this day when fear is gripping hearts,
Causing anguish and stress,
There's still a healing balm at Calvary,
As we turn to God and confess...
Confess we just can't handle it alone,
We need His tender love and care;
Confess many times we've lived as though
The Saviour wasn't even there.
Emotions merely turned inward,
Can cause even more distress,
But when directed to the right source,
Lives can be fully blessed.
It's only in Christ, our precious Lord,
That we find real strength to cope;
His grace is sufficient to calm our fears...
And give us A Glorious Hope!

"Thou art my hope in the day of evil."
"Now the God of hope fill you with all joy and
peace in believing, that ye may abound in hope,
through the power of the Holy Ghost."
(Jer. 17:17; Rom. 15:13)

HE'S COMING VERY SOON

Christ, our Lord, our Glorious King,
Is coming to earth again;
As sure as there's a God in heaven,
It's in His sovereign plan.
No man knows the day or hour,
It could be night or noon,
The signs are clear, the time is near...
He's coming very soon.

Oh, let us work while there's still time
To spread the Gospel seed,
Reaching out to lost hurting souls
In need of being freed.
Time is so short, He's coming soon,
May we, in Him, be found
Obeying the great commission...
When God's great trump shall sound.

Hallelujah! In the twinkling of an eye,
We'll join Him in the air...
What a glorious day that will be
When we shall meet Him there;
It could be today, or tonight,
Tomorrow morn, or noon;
The signs are clear, the time is near...
He's Coming Very Soon!

"And when these things begin to come to pass, then look up,
and lift up your heads; for your redemption draweth nigh."
(Luke 21:28)

PEACE WITH THEE

Lord God, grant true peace in America...
The peace that comes from Thee;
May Thy Spirit move across our great land
Setting the captives free.
Though every foe on this earth be vanquished,
Though all the wars may cease,
Apart from the shed blood of Christ our Lord,
A soul has no true peace.
Oh, may we lift high Thy Royal Banner
For all the world to see...
Only at the cross of Christ our Saviour
Do we find Peace with Thee.

"Therefore being justified by faith,
we have peace with God
through our Lord Jesus Christ"
(Rom. 5:1)

THOSE GREAT TRIALS

In the furnace of that fiery trial,
The Son of God is there...
No need to fear those burning flames
When in His tender care.
And in the den of hungry lions,
He's faithful to His own...
Shutting the mouths of the angry beasts,
Making His presence known.
Oh Friend, what is there ever to fear
When God is on our side?
His Holy Spirit's ever so near
When in Christ we abide.
All enemies are defeated foes
By His amazing grace...
As He reveals Himself in the midst
Of Those Great Trials we face.

"Lo, I see four men loose, walking in the midst
of the fire, and they have no hurt;
and the form of the fourth is like the Son of God."
"My God hath sent his angel, and hath shut
the lions' mouths, that they have not hurt me."
"And no manner of hurt was found upon him,
because he believed in his God."
(Dan. 3:25; 6:22-23)

THANK YOU, LORD

Thank You for times when the sun didn't shine,
Thank You for that cloudy day;
Thank You for troubles and trials I've faced...
It was there I learned to pray.

Thank You for heartaches and lonely nights,
And for those storms I've been through;
Thank You for struggles along the way...
That taught me to trust in You.

Thank You for the dark tunnels of life
When I could not see the end;
Thank You, Lord, for the deepest valleys...
Where I learned You're my best Friend.

Thank You, Lord!

"It is good for me that I have been afflicted;
that I might learn thy statutes."
"O give thanks unto the Lord, for he is good."
(Ps. 119:71; 107:1)

WHEN YOU CAN'T UNDERSTAND

When our finite minds can't understand
The troubles this life doth bring,
Our hearts can know, with full assurance,
The Lord will do the right thing.
We struggle so hard to comprehend
On those rough and stormy days...
But God's thoughts are simply not our thoughts,
And His ways are not our ways.
His intelligence is so much higher
Than what we can understand...
We need only to rest it with Him,
For He has a perfect plan.
If you're struggling to see the reason
For that trial you're going through,
Have faith in God, trust Him completely...
He'll work it out right for you.

"For my thoughts are not your thoughts,
neither are your ways my ways,
saith the Lord. For as the heavens are higher than the earth,
so are my ways higher than your ways,
and my thoughts than your thoughts."
(Is. 55:8-9)

THE VICTORY'S OURS

As sure as our God is working
By His righteous, sovereign hand,
Satan's forces are always there...
Attempting to thwart His plan.
Should we worry or be dismayed
When evil shows its dark face?
Could darkness ever overcome
The light of amazing grace?
If all hell's demons from below
Should run rampant upon earth,
Could one child of God be destroyed
Who's experienced new birth?
While Satan hates God's holiness
And will persist to the end,
Our Creator's so much greater...
The Victory's Ours to win!

"For whatsoever is born of God overcometh the world;
and this is the victory that overcometh
the world, even our faith."
(I John 5:4)

THE KING'S HOLY HIGHWAY

The greatest pleasures in this whole world
Are ours to enjoy each day,
Walking the path of abundant life...
On the King's holy highway.
A path paved with His love, joy and peace,
Longsuffering and gentleness;
With goodness, faith, meekness and temperance,
Security and righteousness.
Such great and glorious blessings are found
By all who travel thereon,
Enjoying the sweet fruit of God's Spirit
As His precious seed is sown.
Our hearts rejoice and sing the vict'ry
Each and every single day,
Walking the path of abundant life...
On The King's Holy Highway.

"As ye have therefore received Christ Jesus
the Lord, so walk ye in him"
"In thy presence is fullness of joy;
at thy right hand there are pleasures for evermore."
(Col. 2:6; Ps. 16:11)

RATHER THAN

I'd rather walk through the valley deep,
Tempted, tested and tried,
Than enjoy the highest mountain peak
Where Satan doth abide.

I'd rather go through rough, deep waters
With Jesus by my side,
Than to sail smoothly on the calm sea
Without His hand to guide.

I'd rather walk in the darkest night
Never seeing ahead,
Than to bask in the brightest sunlight
Where Satan's angels tread.

I'd rather live in the midst of war
With danger all around,
Than to have world peace with compromise –
Truth trampled to the ground.

I'd rather be there on the front line –
A soldier of the cross,
Than never fight the good fight of faith,
And suffer eternal loss.

"Fight the good fight of faith, lay hold on eternal life,
whereunto thou art also called, and hast professed
a good profession before many witnesses."
(I Tim. 6:12)

285

THE GREATEST BLESSINGS

The greatest blessings in all the world
Are the ones that are free:
The sunrise, sunset, the moon and stars,
The beauty of the sea;
A tree, a flower, a falling leaf,
A graceful butterfly,
The melody of a sweet songbird
Soaring through the sky;
The tender touch of a loving hand,
The closeness of a friend,
A compassionate soul reaching out
A helping hand to lend;
Marvelous grace that cleanses the heart,
The privilege of prayer,
The keen awareness of God's presence,
His love and tender care;
The precious gift of His only Son
To redeem you and me...
The Greatest Blessings in all the world
Are the ones that are free.

"Every good gift and every perfect gift is from above,
and cometh down from the Father."
(James 1:17)

THE GREATEST MIRACLE

There's the miracle of creation...
God spake and there was light –
A glorious heavenly sunrise,
The moon and stars at night;
The great magnificent mountains,
The valleys and the plains...
All things were made by God's own hand,
And sovereignly He reigns.
Oh, what a miracle displayed
When, through His Son, He came,
In human form – a virgin birth...
This world's never been the same;
But the Greatest Miracle of all
Is that He loves even me...
He touched my life one glorious day
And set this sinner free!

"God, who is rich in mercy,
for his great love wherewith he loved us,
Even when we were dead in sins,
hath quickened us together with Christ,
(by grace ye are saved)."
(Eph. 2:4-5)

PEACE ON EARTH

The God of all heaven and earth
Has come in human form...
The wise men bowed to worship Him
That great and glorious morn...
A little babe in a manger
With power to change all men...
The son of the living God,
Our Deliverer from sin.
As you worship and adore Him,
Your joy will never cease...
And as your mind is stayed upon Him,
You'll know His perfect peace.

"Glory to God in the highest,
and on earth peace,
good will toward men."
(Luke 2:14)

THE WEIGHT OF SIN

The sin of worry's much too heavy
And not meant for us to bear;
Our great Shephord's there to lift the load...
As we rest it in His care.

The sin of bitterness destroys our joy
And affects the way we live;
It completely steals the victory...
May God help us to forgive.

The sin of pride keeps us from the Lord,
It comes before destruction;
Oh, how we need to humble ourselves...
Obeying God's instruction.

The sin of selfishness grips the soul,
Causing hurt and misery;
Freedom from sin and self can be found...
At the cross of Calvary.

As we come to Christ, heavy laden,
He will cleanse and make us whole;
He'll lift The Weight of Sin completely...
And give sweet rest to the soul.

"Come unto me, all ye that labour and are
heavy laden, and I will give you rest."
"For my yoke is easy, and my burden is light."
(Matt. 11:28, 30)

PRECIOUS NAME

There is a name so precious
Angels worship at the sound;
No greater name on this earth,
Or in heaven can be found.
The precious name of Jesus
Melts the heart of sinful man;
Every knee shall bow to Him
At the end of times great span.
Oh, that all would bow today
And seal their spiritual fate,
Rising to new life in Him
Before it is too late.
It's through His precious blood
The path to heaven's paved...
No other name is given
Whereby we must be saved.
For this eternal purpose,
The Lord and Saviour came,
Purchasing our pardon...
JESUS, what a Precious Name!

"Thou shalt call his name JESUS:
for he shall save his people from their sins."
"There is none other name under heaven
given among men, whereby we must be saved."
(Matt. 1:21; Acts 4:12)

PRECIOUS PROMISES

Through the valleys of fiery trials,
God holds us in His hand...
His great and precious promises
Forevermore shall stand.
Souls who bow before the Saviour,
Receiving Holy Seed,
Are promised all sufficient grace
For every single need.

Each trial and hardship that we face
Must first go through God's hand...
We can rest on His promises
When we don't understand.
He promised to take care of us
As we trust and obey,
He'll never leave nor forsake us...
He's with us every day.

When surrendered to God's keeping,
We'll always have His best...
Resting on precious promises,
Our hearts are fully blessed.
He can be trusted completely
Every promise to keep,
Including the greatest of all...
Eternal life to reap.

Such great and Precious Promises!

"Whereby are given unto us exceeding great and precious promises:
that by these ye might be partakers of the divine nature,
having escaped the corruption that is in the world through lust."
(II Pet. 1:4)

TRANSLATED INTO HIS KINGDOM

Translated into God's Kingdom
Through a new spiritual birth,
Abundant life in Christ is ours
Right here upon the earth.
Into our hearts His Spirit came,
Where once was darkness grim,
Imparting fruits of righteousness...
Love, joy and peace in Him,
A life of communion with God
As we walk in His way,
Prayer and worship with His people
As we serve Him each day.
Life in His glorious Kingdom
Is one of victory,
As we praise our loving Saviour
For setting our souls free.
And when we reach our home above
To live forevermore,
We'll praise Him through eternity
On that celestial shore.

"Giving thanks unto the Father... Who hath
delivered us from the power of darkness,
and translated us into the kingdom of his dear Son."
(Col. 1:12-13)

THE MASTER'S VINEYARD

When you toil in the Master's vineyard,
He is with you everyday,
Giving you strength and grace sufficient
For hardships along the way;
And when you become discouraged,
Thinking all you do's in vain,
His loving hand is there to lift you
To an even higher plain.

If you should feel you have no talent,
And there's just no work for you,
Look on the fields ready to harvest,
You'll see something you can do.
Oh, let God use you in His vineyard,
Where folks need His loving care,
As you reach out to help another...
You will find your own growth there.

"Lift up your eyes, and look on the fields;
for they are white already to harvest."
"Grow in grace, and in the knowledge of
our Lord and Saviour Jesus Christ.
To him be glory both now and forever. Amen."
(John 4:35; II Pet. 3:18)

GOD IS THERE FOR YOU

When dreams are shattered by circumstance,
And it seems all hope is gone...
When you've trusted in mere luck and chance,
And you feel so all alone...
God is There for You.

When you've exhausted every resource,
And you think you've reached the end...
When you just don't know which way to turn,
He's your closest, dearest friend...
And He Cares for You.

When those best made plans, you thought so right,
Have turned out to be so wrong...
Our Great Shepherd's there to lead the way,
With a new and glorious song...
He Abides with You.

As you follow Christ in all you do,
When you fail, you still succeed...
He gives you the desires of your heart,
And supplies your every need...
He Provides for You.

So when you feel that you have no hope,
And that nothing's going right...
Just focus your eyes on the Saviour,
And walk by faith – not by sight...
God is There for You!

"Delight thyself also in the Lord;
and he shall give thee the desires of thine heart."
"Casting all your care upon him; for he careth for you."
(Ps. 37:4; I Pet. 5:7)

GOD, GIVE US CHRISTIANS!

God, give us Christians on fire for You,
With unwavering faith, tried and true...
Christians unafraid to take a stand
Against the wiles of Satan's hand;
Clothed in Your armor, ready to fight
For all that's good, sacred and right;
Christians kind, yet not willing to bend
Your precious Truth for foe nor friend,
Planted firmly on the solid Rock,
Unyielding to the tempter's knock.
Christians pure in heart and strong in mind,
Delivered from sin's chains that bind,
Mighty in Spirit and hand in hand...
Can make a difference in this land.
God, Give Us Christians!

"Be strong in the Lord, and in the power of his might.
Put on the whole armour of God, that ye
may be able to stand against the wiles of the devil."
(Eph. 6:10-11)

THE TEST OF CHRISTIANITY

It's such a wonderful Christian life
When all is going our way,
The church bells ringing, the great choir singing,
Oh, what a glorious day!
But when troubles come and doubts arise,
And we feel so all alone,
Can we still rejoice? Do we hear God's voice
Assuring us we're His own?

It's easy to walk the walk of faith
When the devil's far behind;
Focused upon Christ, we're just not enticed
To fall into sins that bind;
But when Satan's near, clouding our view,
Alluring our hearts to stray,
It is then we know, for our actions show,
Just who we serve and obey.

In the depths of sorrow and suffering,
Is our faith in God still strong?
Can we still proclaim His glorious Name
When everything's going wrong?
The true test of Christianity
Is in the dark, stormy vale...
The faith that survives is that which relies
On Christ... He will never fail.

eloved, think it not strange concerning the fiery trial which is to try you...
But rejoice, inasmuch as ye are partakers of Christ's sufferings."
"Let us hold fast the profession of our faith without wavering;
(for he is faithful that promised)"
(I Pet. 4:12, 13; Heb. 10:23)

EVIDENCE OF THINGS NOT SEEN

Though our eyes can't see the wind,
We can feel it as it blows;
We cannot tell whence it comes,
Nor just how or where it goes;
Yet, the strong, tall trees are bent,
Quiet waters tempest tossed;
Houses built upon the sand...
Can result in total loss.
Though we cannot see the wind
As it whistles through the air,
The effects are clearly seen...
There's no doubt that it is there.

Though our eyes can't see God's Spirit,
We can feel His presence near;
Somehow He touches our lives
Calming our innermost fear.
The strong and proud are humbled,
Hearts cleansed and freed from sin;
Houses built upon the Rock...
Are safe and secure within.
Though we cannot see God's Spirit
As He moves upon our soul,
The effects are clearly seen...
There's no doubt He makes us whole!

"The wind bloweth where it listeth, and thou hearest the sound thereof
but canst not tell whence it cometh, and whither it goeth:
so is every one that is born of the Spirit."
(John 3:8)

COME TO CHRIST TODAY

Come and kneel before the Saviour now,
He's just too precious not to bow...
He's reaching out to you dear friend.
His Spirit has called to you before,
Oh, do not linger anymore...
Come to Christ and be freed from sin.

God's amazing grace is yours to have,
In Him you'll find a healing salve...
Your wounded heart He'll take and mend.
His Word's too powerful not to heed,
It's milk and meat your soul to feed...
It is your shield and strength within.

Come bow at the cross and be made whole,
Abundant joy will fill your soul...
You'll have peace that will never end.
Heaven's just too glorious to miss,
Eternal life in perfect bliss...
Oh, Come to Christ Today my friend.

"Behold now is the accepted time;
behold, now is the day of salvation."
(II Cor. 6:2)

LEST I FALL AWAY

Oh God, any message You'd send through me,
I pray You'd strongly preach to me...
For I know there's the possibility
I would miss what You'd say to me.
Keep me true in times of prosperity
When I tend to wander from Thee;
And those days when all just seems to go wrong,
Give me a faith that's real and strong;
Help me to trust Your hand of sovereignty
When my eyes cannot clearly see.
Lord, should You send a Faith Message today,
Preach it to me... Lest I Fall Away.

Paul said: "I keep under my body,
and bring it into subjection: lest that by any means,
when I have preached to others,
I myself should be a castaway."
(I Cor. 9:27)

THE LIGHT WITHIN

The Light of Christ, our Lord who came,
Burns bright within the soul
Of all who bear His precious Name,
Forgiven and made whole.
Oh, do not let your Light grow dim,
Walk in His righteous way;
Just keep your eyes focused on Him
And serve Him every day.
As you feed on His Holy Word,
Praising His wondrous Name,
Within your heart and soul is stirred,
A warm and glowing flame.
Oh, let it shine forever bright
In this dark world about...
That others may behold the Light
That never shall go out.

Jesus said: "Ye are the light of the world."
"Let your light so shine before men, that they may see
your good works, and glorify your Father which is in heaven."
(Matt. 5:14, 16)

WHEN GOD LEADS, HE WILL PROVIDE

When God brings us to green pastures,
Such wondrous blessings unfold,
As He leads beside still waters
And restores the weary soul.

And when He leads through the desert,
He protects us from the heat,
As He brings us to the fountain
Of pure water... oh, so sweet.

When our Lord leads through the valley,
He is right there by our side,
And in the darkest stormy night...
He's our Light and loving Guide.

And when He leads through rough waters,
Where turbulent waves are steep,
And we feel we'll sink and perish...
He carries us through the deep.

When you can't see the way ahead,
Just follow the Shepherd's guide;
Never fear what the future holds...
When God Leads... He Will Provide!

"The Lord is my shepherd; I shall not want."
(Ps. 23:1)

TOUCHED WITH OUR INFIRMITIES

God is not a harsh, distant Father,
Untouched by our infirmities,
But He's a tender loving Shepherd
Who's with us through adversities.
Christ was tempted on earth as we are,
Yet remained Holy... without sin;
The great God of all the universe,
Is our closest and dearest friend.
He understands all that we go through
And is right there to undergird,
Giving strength and grace in time of need,
Feeding our spirit with His Word.
Oh, Let us praise His wonderful Name,
He always hears and answers prayer,
For He's Touched With Our Infirmities...
A God of mercy, love and care.

"For we have not an high priest which cannot be
touched with the feeling of our infirmities;
but was in all points tempted like as we are, yet without sin.
Let us therefore come boldly unto
the throne of grace, that we may obtain mercy,
and find grace to help in time of need."
(Heb. 4:15, 16)

TOUCHED BY THE MASTER'S HAND

The leper was healed and made clean,
But just how he could not tell,
He only knew the Master's hand
Had touched him and made him well.
Just how my Lord could cleanse my heart
I will never understand,
But this one thing I truly know...
I've been touched by the Master's hand.

The blind man could not understand
How Christ healed him with mere clay,
But He knew without any doubt
He'd received his sight that day.
Just how He opened my blind eyes
I will never understand,
But this one thing I truly know...
I've been touched by the Master's hand.

Lazarus was touched and brought to life
When the Saviour called his name,
He came forth from the grave that day,
Nevermore to be the same.
Just why my Lord would save my soul
I will never understand,
But this one thing I truly know...
I've been touched by the Master's hand.

I've been touched by the Master's hand,
And I just can't understand
Why He loves me so, I only know...
I've Been Touched By The Master's Hand.

"And Jesus, moved with compassion, put forth his hand,
and touched him... and he was cleansed."
(Mark 1:41, 42)

TAKE MY HAND, LORD

When everything is going well
And happiness and joy prevail...
Take my hand, Lord, keep me true;
And when my world just falls apart,
And I suffer a broken heart...
Take my hand, Lord, lead me through.

When sickness comes and I am weak,
And the future looks dark and bleak...
Your healing hand strengthens me;
And when I've lost someone who's dear,
My soul engulfed in grief and fear...
Your hand alone comforts me.

When tried, and tempted to give up,
Your touch just always fills my cup...
Take my hand, Lord, guide me on;
And when this life on earth is o'er
And I am facing heaven's shore...
Take My Hand, Lord... lead me home.

"If I take the wings of the morning, and dwell in the uttermost
parts of the sea; Even there shall thy hand lead me,
and thy right hand shall hold me."
(Ps. 139:9-10)

UNTIL THEN

When my work on earth is over,
Lord, just take my feeble hand,
Lead me to my home in glory –
That celestial Promise Land...
But Until Then, may Thy Spirit
Set my heart and soul on fire
With the flame of Thy great gospel,
The lost and weak to inspire.

When my life here draws to a close,
And I can serve Thee no more,
Lord, take me to my heavenly home –
That glorious, peaceful shore...
But Until Then, with thanksgiving,
I will live my life for Thee,
And pray my light would brightly burn,
For lost, hurting souls to see.

"Let your loins be girded about, and your lights burning;
"Be ye therefore ready also: for the Son of man cometh
at an hour when ye think not."
(Luke 12:35, 40)

SURRENDER ALL

Christ surrendered all on the cross;
He bore our sin and shame,
That we might never suffer loss,
Oh, Praise His Glorious Name!

I could never thank Him enough
For what He did for me;
His blood washed all my sin away
And set this prisoner free.

A million years would be too few
To praise my God and King,
I can only surrender all...
My heart and soul I bring.

He gave His all for you, my friend,
Just hear His tender call...
His blood will cleanse you from your sin
As you Surrender All.

"In whom we have redemption through
his blood, the forgiveness of sins,
according to the riches of his grace"
(Eph. 1:7)

WHILE THERE'S STILL TIME

Whatever we do for God,
We must do while there's still time...
Time to thank that faithful friend
Who's been so helpful and kind;
Time to return a favor
And just go the extra mile;
Time to reach out to others
With a warm handshake or smile;
Time to love one another
And help out when there's a need;
Time to join hands together
And spread the gospel seed;
Time to tell this whole wide world
Of God's great redemption plan;
Time to let our light so shine
That it reaches every man;
Time to Praise God, the Father,
For the work that He has done;
Time to rejoice evermore
In our Saviour, Christ, the Son.
Time is just so important
And we make more than we find...
Whatever we do for God,
Let us do While There's Still Time.

"See then that ye walk circumspectly, not as fools, but as wise,
redeeming the time, because the days are evil."
(Eph. 5:15-16)

NO OTHER FRIEND LIKE JESUS

There's just no other friend like Jesus...
On the cross He gave His all;
He's so much closer than a brother
And can always hear our call.
In troubled waters, His hand guides us
And carries us through the deep;
From the enemy, His arm hides us...
He always protects His sheep.
He cares about all that we go through,
His love is beyond compare;
He'll never leave us, nor forsake us...
When we need Him, He's right there.
Who else could ever be so faithful?
Who could ever take His place?
There's just No Other Friend Like Jesus...
One day we'll behold His face.

"There is a friend that sticketh closer than a brother."
"... our Lord Jesus, that great shepherd of the sheep..."
"And his servants shall serve him: and they shall see his face."
(Prov. 18:24; Heb. 13:20; Rev. 22:3-4)

DO WE LOVE HIM?

Do we love our Saviour...
Our great Shepherd and King?
Then let us feed His lambs,
And lost ones to Him bring.

Do we really love Him
With all our heart and soul?
Then let us feed His sheep...
Reach out to young and old.

Do we truly love Christ?
Have we surrendered all?
Then let us feed His sheep...
Oh, hear the Master's call.

"Jesus saith to Simon Peter... lovest thou me more than these?
He saith unto him, Yea, Lord; thou knowest that I love thee.
He saith unto him, Feed my lambs. Feed my sheep."
And again: "Jesus saith unto him, Feed my sheep."
(John 21:15-17)

A VOICE IN THE WILDERNESS

As Christians obey the great commission,
Fulfilling God's purpose and plan,
A voice still cries out in the wilderness...
"Repent: the kingdom of heaven's at hand."

What a joy to share the gospel of Christ
And see God's Spirit change a man;
What a privilege it is to carry
Our Lord's message throughout the land.

Thank You, Father, that we can be a part
Of Your redemption plan on earth,
And witness the power of salvation...
As a soul is given new birth.

May we always be about Your business,
Sharing Christ with our fellowman,
A voice crying out in the wilderness...
"Repent: the kingdom of heaven's at hand."

"John the Baptist, preaching in the wilderness of Judaea,
And saying, Repent ye: for the kingdom of heaven is at hand."
Jesus said: "... except ye repent, ye shall all likewise perish."
(Matt. 3:1-2; Luke 13:3)

IF I'D NEVER SEEN

If I'd never seen an answered prayer,
I'd just keep praying even more;
I know whatever God does is best
As He leads me to heaven's shore.
If I'd never seen a dream come true,
I'd keep on dreaming anyway;
I don't have to see a sign to know
Miracles happen every day.

If I'd never seen a single sheep
Brought into the glorious fold,
I'd just keep on sowing gospel seed
Till my Shepherd's face I behold.
If I'd not seen a beautiful rose
Among the thorns of test and trial,
I'd still want to live and love and give,
Praising my Saviour all the while.

I've seen so many answers to prayer,
My Lord has always brought me through,
And so many of the dreams I've dreamed
Have miraculously come true.
I've seen souls brought into the Kingdom
As we've sown precious gospel seed;
I've enjoyed the beauty of roses,
My God has more than met my need!

But If I'd Never Seen anything...
I'd still worship my precious Lord;
I would give Him Glory every day
And just depend upon His Word;
I'd sing and shout and I'd praise His Name;
I'd trust Him, pray, and even dream,
And reaching out to needy souls...
I'd smell the roses never seen.

"Jesus saith unto him, Thomas, because thou hast seen me,
thou hast believed: blessed are they that have not seen,
and yet have believed."
(John 20:29)

FISHERS OF MEN

Right where we are, on the sea of life,
Our Lord calls us from all sin...
And as we leave our nets and follow,
He makes us fishers of men.

Men, bound in the sea of destruction,
Struggle on the gospel line...
Some get away and fall by the side,
The new life never to find;
Others grasp the precious gospel Truth,
And are brought out of death's sea...
Praising the Saviour for life anew,
Their souls now cleansed and made free.

The loving Master's most tender call
Can be clearly heard within...
"My children, leave it all, follow me,
I'll make you Fishers of Men."

Jesus said: "Follow me, and I will make you fishers of men.
And they straightway left their nets, and followed him."
(Matt. 4:19-20)

I BELIEVE

I believe Christ, the Son of the Living God,
Came down to earth;
I believe He died for sin and rose again
To give new birth;
I believe He lives today and sets men free
To live with Him eternally...
Yes, I believe!

I believe that in the very darkest night,
He is our Light;
I believe when traveling on life's roughest road,
He lifts our load;
I believe if we'll just look to Him each day,
He'll take our hand and lead the way...
Yes, I believe!

I believe when all hope is beyond our view,
He sees us through;
I believe miracles can happen every day,
If we'll just pray;
I believe our Lord, who came to save lost man,
Will soon return to earth again...
Yes, I believe!

I believe we'll see Him coming in the air
And meet Him there;
I believe we'll dwell with Him on heaven's shore
Forevermore.
Every time I see the twinkling stars come out,
Or view the moon, I want to shout...
Oh, how I Believe!

"He that believeth on the Son hath everlasting life:
and he that believeth not the Son shall not see life;
but the wrath of God abideth on him."
(John 3:36)

I AM NOT ASHAMED

I am not ashamed to take a stand
For Christ, my Lord and King,
And spread His gospel through the Land,
For He's my everything!

I am not ashamed to worship Him
And lift His name on high...
My soul's redeemed from darkness grim,
His Truth I can't deny.

I am not ashamed to stand my ground
Out on the battlefield,
Though Satan's forces may surround,
I have a mighty Shield.

Having died for sin, Christ rose again,
And oh, what joy He gives...
I Am Not Ashamed to proclaim,
I'll tell the world He lives!

"I am not ashamed of the gospel of Christ:
for it is the power of God
unto salvation to everyone that believeth."
(Rom. 1:16)

NOT BY BREAD ALONE

The greatest blessings in our lives...
The abundant joy we've known,
The peace and love within our hearts,
Do not come by bread alone.

The material things we possess...
The money, houses and land,
Are just trinkets upon life's shore,
Soon blown away in the sand.

But the true riches of God's grace
Remain forever our own...
Abundant life, joy, peace and love,
Are given by Christ alone.

Mere bread could never satisfy
The hunger within our hearts,
Nor could those things which we possess
Give the joy our Lord imparts.

God sends down manna from heaven,
As His Word in us is sown,
Feeding our souls forevermore...
We live... Not By Bread Alone.

Jesus said: "It is written, Man shall not live by bread alone,
but by every word that proceedeth out of the mouth of God."
(Matt. 4:4)

A PLACE OF BEGINNING AGAIN

There is a place to be found by man,
A wonderful, peaceful shore,
A place where one can begin again...
A clean slate forevermore.
A place where sin is taken away
And replaced with righteousness,
As repentant souls bow down to pray
Receiving God's holiness.

It's found at the foot of the cruel cross
Of Christ Jesus, Lord and King,
The One who paid the ultimate cost,
Salvation by grace to bring.
There's no other place in all this world
That provides such hope for man,
Oh, what a heavenly sweet retreat...
A Place of Beginning Again.

"If we confess our sins, he is faithful and just to forgive us
our sins, and to cleanse us from all unrighteousness."
"Thou, Lord, art good, and ready to forgive."
(I John 1:9; Ps. 86:5)

THE ONLY WAY

There's no other way to the Father
But through His only Son...
No other way to enter heaven
When time on earth is done;
No other way to have forgiveness,
And a new spiritual birth;
No other way to abundant life
As we live here on earth.

Only in Christ is that true joy found
Many are searching for...
He gives real peace and satisfaction,
And He's the only door.
Come kneel at the cross of Calvary,
He'll cleanse and make you free;
Come and taste the honey in the rock,
And feed eternally.

Though the pathway is straight and narrow,
With many trials and tests,
Heavenly manna from the Father
Brings life that's truly blest.
The foretaste of Glory imparted
Gives vict'ry every day
To the soul surrendered to Jesus...
He is The Only Way!

"Jesus saith unto him, I am the way, the truth, and the life:
no man cometh unto the Father, but by me."
"I am come that they might have life,
and that they might have it more abundantly."
(John 14:6; John 10:10)

AS THE MOON RISES

As the moon rises o'er the mountain
And the stars so brightly glisten,
The voice of our Maker can be heard
By all who prayerfully listen.

His message is spoken so clearly
To the humble heart of man...
"I am the Lord thy God... Creator;
I have formed thee by my hand;
I hung the moon there in the heavens
And put each star in its place;
I sent my only begotten Son
To redeem thee by my grace.
My Spirit calls out to one and all...
'Come to Christ, receive new birth;'
What more could I do to show my love
To all people on the earth?"

As The Moon Rises o'er the mountain
And the stars so brightly glisten,
The voice of our Maker can be heard
By all who prayerfully listen.

Thus saith the Lord: "I have made the earth, and created man upon it:
I, even my hands, have stretched out the heavens,
and all their host have I commanded."
"I have loved thee with an everlasting love;
therefore with loving kindness have I drawn thee."
"He that hath ears to hear, let him hear."
(Is. 45:12; Jer. 31:3; Matt. 11:15)

LIFT UP YOUR EYES

Lift up your eyes unto the hills
And seek the Father above...
The Great God of all creation
Reveals His mercy and love.

Lift up your eyes to Calvary
Where Christ gave His life that day...
No greater love was ever shown
Than on that hill far away.

Lift your eyes to the empty tomb,
There you'll see the Risen King...
Bow down and worship the Saviour,
Arise and joyfully sing.

View the clouds where He ascended
And shall one day come again...
Lift up your eyes unto the hills,
Help comes from God's loving hand.

"I will lift up mine eyes unto the hills,
from whence cometh my help.
My help cometh from the Lord,
which made heaven and earth."
(Ps. 121:1-2)

TRUE PEACE

Often we look to circumstance
To bring contentment and peace,
Only to find disappointment
When our problems do not cease.
True peace comes not from this world,
But from God and God alone,
As we come to know Christ Jesus
Who redeems us for His own.
Forgiven of sin and made clean,
What wondrous peace we find...
Peace that passes understanding,
Beyond the human mind.

Father, thank you that as we walk
In fellowship with Thee,
True Peace flows from Thy Throne above,
And reaches even me.

"The Lord will bless his people with peace."
"And the peace of God, which passeth all understanding,
shall keep your hearts and minds through Christ Jesus."
(Ps. 29:11; Phil. 4:7)

Prayer Messages

"Not forsaking the assembling of ourselves together…"
(Hebrews 10:25)

D.D.W

Prayer Messages

Sweet Hour of Prayer

My Prayer

The Holy One

Take My Life

Prepare Us for Service

Search Me

May We Never Waiver

Strengthen Us Lord

Slow Us Down

When Do I Need Thee

Make Us Your Vessels

Oh How We Worship You

Empty Me

Fill Me

MY PRAYER

Lord, on that old rugged cross of Calvary,
You shed your blood and suffered agony.
You were mocked, scorned and spat upon,
By those who denied You were God's own Son;
But the Father had a purpose, it's plain to see –
You arose from the tomb with great victory.
You conquered death, hell and the grave,
For a sinner's soul such as mine to save.
Then one day You called to me
To take up my cross and follow Thee.
That glorious day You cleansed my heart –
A brand new life You did impart.
I thank You, Lord, for redeeming me,
And if I had but one prayer, that prayer would be...
"Lord, keep me ever yielded to Thee."

"Yield yourselves unto God,
as those that are alive from the dead."
(Rom. 6:13)

THE HOLY ONE

Thou art the Holy One, God of the universe,
Creator of all art Thou.
Holy, Holy, Holy, Lord God Almighty,
All heaven and earth shall bow.
Such a mighty God, yet our loving Father,
Lord, how can it be?
You sent Your Son to shed his blood,
To cleanse and make us free.
Keep me on the narrow way,
Oh, Shepherd of my soul,
And if I should stray, reach out I pray,
And draw me back into Thy fold.
Lord, as Thou art Holy, make me holy too,
That as I walk with Thee each day...
My life would glorify You.

"The Holy One of Israel is our King.
"Glorify God in your body, and in your spirit,
which are God's."
(Ps. 89:18; I Cor. 6:20)

TAKE MY LIFE

Take my life and let it be
Consecrated, Lord, to Thee.
May all I do and all I say
Bring glory and honor to Thee today.
Mold me and make me as You would have me to be,
That Your light would shine forth for others to see...
Christ is the answer for heartache and sin –
Such a need in this world for cleansing within.
Begin, Oh, Lord, in me I pray,
Then reach out to others who have gone astray.
Make me a vessel, pure and true,
With one goal in mind, to glorify You...
And when I would tend to wander away,
Remind me, Lord, to kneel and pray...
For I don't want to live for self again,
Having been delivered by Thine own hand.
So, take my life and let it be,
Consecrated Lord to Thee.

"Present your bodies a living sacrifice,
holy, acceptable unto God."
(Rom. 12:1)

PREPARE US FOR SERVICE

Father, prepare us for Your service we pray...
May our lives glorify You each day.
Give us clean hands and a pure heart,
And in Your kingdom may we do our part
To be used of You in some small way,
Ministering to those who've gone astray.
Oh God, work through us, some soul to win
Whose life is broken and lost in sin;
Prepare us to be Your instruments of peace,
In a world of turmoil and wars without cease.
May we always submit to Your control,
As You gently prod within the fold;
And the times we need a firmer hand,
We pray You'd harshly reprimand.
Take us and mold us into the image of Your Son...
Preparing us for the race You'd have us run.
Fill us with Your Holy Spirit we humbly ask,
Enabling us to meet our daily tasks.
Help us to labor for the things of eternity,
Shunning the world of frivolity,
For we want to be faithful servants to You,
Following Your guidance in all that we do.
It's by Your Spirit the victory is won,
And all praise and honor goes to Your Son...
Our Lord and Saviour who made the way
For us to dwell in heaven with You someday.

Christ himself came not to be served, but to reach out,
Teaching us what serving is all about.
Help us follow His steps and serve compassionately,
As wo oce the needs wherever they be;
And at the end when the race has been run,
Father, may we hear Your voice say... "Well Done."

"For even the Son of man came
not to be ministered unto, but to minister"
(Mark 10:45)

SEARCH ME

Search me, oh Lord, and reveal to me
Some wicked way I fail to see.
Show me the things that I've done wrong,
Those hidden things that don't belong,
Not just the hurt I've caused someone,
But all the things I should have done...
The sins of omission –
As well as commission.
Help me to see from Thy holy view –
The things I should and shouldn't do.
Surface my sins, make them clear and plain,
Let not one ugly spot remain;
Then convict me of each one I see,
That I might humbly bow before Thee.
Grant true repentance as I confess,
Seeking Your mercy and forgiveness;
Cleanse me of every sin I pray,
And help me to walk the righteous way.
The desire of my heart is to live for You,
Abiding by Your word in all that I do;
So, Search Me Dear Lord, and purify me...
That my life would bring glory and honor to Thee.

"Search me, oh God, and know my heart."
(Ps. 139:23)

MAY WE NEVER WAIVER

Lord, help us to be good, honest and true,
Seeking Your will in all that we do.
May we never waiver the teachings we've heard,
Preached and taught from Your Holy Word.
You've given instructions and commandments so clear,
And our lives will be blessed if only we'll hear.
As we bow in submission, Your word comes alive,
Feeding our hearts, our souls to revive.
So, may we never waiver, but remain ever true –
Solid and steadfast in all that we do.

"Be ye steadfast, unmovable, always abounding
in the work of the Lord."
(I Cor. 15:58)

STRENGTHEN US LORD

Strengthen us, Lord, for the days ahead –
The loss of loved ones – our deepest dread.
Heartache and pain are sure to come
When those close depart for their heavenly home.
Though we know they go to a much better place,
We survive the hurt only by Your grace.
Help us rely on Your tender care,
As You reach out in love, our grief to bear.
It's these difficult times You carry us through,
Teaching us to depend solely on You;
So strengthen us, Lord, prepare our heart
To lean on You when loved ones depart.

"The Lord is my strength and my shield;
my heart trusted in him, and I am helped."
(Ps. 28:7)

SLOW US DOWN

Slow us down Lord, we're moving too fast.
Help us to smell the roses while they last,
And enjoy each blessing of every day,
As we walk with You along life's way.
May we never rush on out ahead,
But always follow Your lead instead.
Too often we miss Your very best
As we hurry through life thinking we're blest.
Those temporal things we work so hard for
Seem only to leave us wanting more.
The harder we work, the faster we go,
And the more we have, the less we know.
When we do slow down and breathe a sigh,
We find there's more to life than meets the eye –
Spiritual things that fill our soul,
Satisfy our hearts and make us whole.
It's those every day blessings we sometimes miss
That give us joy and heavenly bliss...
So, slow us down Lord, and enable us to see
Each and every blessing that comes from Thee.

"Wait on the Lord: be of good courage,
and He shall strengthen thine heart:
wait I say, on the Lord."
(Ps. 27:14)

WHEN DO I NEED THEE?

It's not just every month of every single year,
Or when life's turmoils cause my heart to fear.
And it's not just every day of every single week,
Or when a special need causes me to seek.
Nor is it just every hour of every single day,
Or when I stumble along life's way...
Oh, God, it's not just in these times I need Your
grace and power...
But it's every single moment of every single hour.

"As the hart panteth after the water brooks,
so panteth my soul after Thee, Oh God."
(Ps. 42:1)

MAKE US YOUR VESSELS

Father, make us Your vessels, pure and clean,
Reaching out to the lost and needy,
Living our lives in service for Thee,
Rather than selfish and greedy.
What a joy and privilege to do Your will,
As we walk in fellowship with You –
Serving, witnessing, obeying Your Word,
In everything we do;
And when we fail along the way
To do what You have asked,
We know You choose another
To accomplish Your purpose and task –
But then we're the ones who suffer loss,
And miss Your very best;
For as You use us in Your kingdom,
Our hearts are truly blessed.
So help us to see that when we serve others
You give us even more,
And Make Us Your Vessels each day we live...
Till we reach eternity's door.

"If any man serve me, let him follow me;
and where I am there shall my servant be:
If any man serve me, him will my Father honour."
(John 12:26)

OH HOW WE WORSHIP YOU

You're The Alpha and Omega –
The beginning and the end,
The Almighty God of the universe,
And our closest, dearest Friend.
You're The Everlasting Father,
The Ruler of all the earth,
The Son who came in the flesh
That we might have new birth.
You're The Rock of all ages,
The Bright and Morning Star,
Our Great and Mighty Fortress –
We glory in Who You Are.
You're our Lord and Master;
We've heard Your sovereign call,
And bowed in faith, repenting,
Surrendering to You... our all.
Now as we lift our voice on high
In humble adoration,
Our hearts overflow with praise,
And joyful celebration.
You've redeemed our sinful souls,
Giving us life anew;
You're our eternal King Of Glory...
Oh How We Worship You.

"O come, let us worship and bow down: let us kneel before
the Lord our maker. For He is our God; and we are
the people of His pasture, and the sheep of His hand."
(Ps. 95:6, 7)

EMPTY ME

Heavenly Father, I pray You'd empty me
Of every unclean thing You see.
Take away all my sin and pride,
And make me pure and clean inside.
A vessel must be empty
For Your Holy Spirit to fill,
So, Empty Me of all but Thee,
That I might do Thy will.

"But we have this treasure in earthen vessels,
that the excellency of the power
may be of God, not of us."
(II Cor. 4:7)

FILL ME

Oh, God, fill me with Thy Holy Spirit –
Thy precious Heavenly Dove.
May Thy sweet presence fill my cup
With joyful praise and love.
Then when my cup is full
Of heavenly fruits and glory,
Use me to pass the message on,
Of the old redemption story.
God, forbid that I should keep
Such treasure hidden in my soul,
But present my body a living sacrifice,
That others be made whole.
So Fill Me, Father, with Thy Holy Spirit,
And may my cup overflow…
Spilling out on all around,
That others, Thy Son, would know.

"Being filled with the fruits of righteousness,
which are by Jesus Christ,
unto the glory and praise of God."
(Phil. 1:11)

Personal Messages

"The very hairs of your head are all numbered."
(Matthew 10:30)

Personal Messages

His Eye is on the Sparrow

REVELATION

I searched and searched, but couldn't find
Contentment or real peace of mind.
My soul cried out in darkness and fear
For the truth of God and to feel him near.
Then God in his mercy reached down from above,
And revealed in a moment his wonderful love.
Through Jesus the Master I'm saved by his grace,
And know that some day I shall look on his face.
No more will I search, for my soul has been fed...
Never to wander, by him I am led.

"By grace are ye saved through faith;
and that not of yourselves:
it is the gift of God: Not of works,
lest any man should boast."
(Eph. 2:8-9)

THAT'S LOVE

To reach down and redeem a wretch such as I,
And give me new life when I deserved to die...
That's love.
To make me His child, His very own,
And bless me with joy like I've never known...
That's love.
To forgive and forget when I go astray,
And be there each time to show me the way...
That's love.
To open my eyes so that I may see
The truth of His Word revealed to me...
That's love.
To bleed, to suffer and then to die,
To make this life possible for such as I...
That's Love... That's Love.

"Herein is love, not that we loved God,
but that He loved us,
and sent his Son to be
the propitiation for our sins."
(I John 4:10)

A LOVE STORY

I never knew love until I met You...
You're the one that completes my soul.
Other times I thought love was real,
Even vowed to have and to hold;
Yet, it wasn't long as time went by,
The magical flame went out.
Little did I know in days of old
What real love was all about.
You've satisfied my deepest longings,
Rejoiced my lonely heart.
You're the one for whom I've searched
Right from the very start.
Everything my heart desires
Is satisfied in You;
And every dream I've ever dreamed
Has now at last come true.
Your strength, Your goodness, Your tender care –
Such love – how can it be?
Dear Lord above, You're always there,
And You're everything to me.

"Thou shalt love the Lord thy God with all thy heart,
and all thy soul, and with all thy mind."
(Matt. 22:37)

Follow by reading: "A Soul Mate"

A SOUL MATE

We meet the One for Whom we've searched
When entering the spiritual birth...
Then the heavenly Father blesses our life
With a soul mate here on earth.
Blessing after blessing shared,
Together as husband and wife...
Following our Lord and Saviour,
Weathering the storms of life.
Whatever trials may come our way,
However large or small,
Our God is with us every day,
Sufficient to meet them all.
As we look to Him in all we do,
Our burdens on Him to cast...
His strength will surely see us through,
And our marriage will always last.
Such a marvelous gift, this sacred bond,
Given by the Father above...
Sanctioned by His grace and power,
Infused with His great love.
Heavenly sweet communion,
Shared by woman and man.
Holy blissful union,
According to His plan.
Not merely luck,
More than just fate –
God's divine providence...
A Soul Mate.

"Marriage is honourable in all"
(Heb. 13:4)

346

A WALK ON THE ROAD

There's a country road I walk each day –
It's a beautiful shady lane;
And as I walk I often pray...
Lord, make Your will for me plain.
The woodland animals, the birds of the air,
All know just what to do.
Sometimes I wonder, Lord, are they
Much closer than I to You?
But, when I continue to look about,
Rejoicing floods my soul,
And convicted I stand of any doubt,
For I know You're in control.
As I consider the lilies of the field,
There's neither toil nor strife.
Your grace provides for all who yield,
Directing and guiding their life.
So help me, Lord, to rest in You,
And trust You all the way.
Then I, too, will know just what to do...
As I walk the road each day.

"Trust in the Lord with all thine heart;
In all thy ways acknowledge him,
and he shall direct thy paths."
(Prov. 3:5-6)

347

CHRISTIAN POETS NEVER DIE

Christian poets never die, they just write away:
Should e'er it be they could not write,
They'd just speak what they have to say;
And should it be they could not speak,
Sign language would do each day;
And should they have no hands to sign
What's on their hearts to convey,
They'd simply meditate day and night,
And tell it to God as they pray.
And when they leave the beauty here
For heaven's bright array,
On the other side of the starry sky
In that new and glorious day,
There's sure to be a pen, just for them,
To say what they must say...
Christian poets never die, they just write away.

"I will speak of the glorious honour of thy majesty,
and of thy wondrous works."
"My tongue is the pen of a ready writer."
(Ps. 145:5; 45:1)

Connie Campbell Bratcher was born in Atlanta, Georgia, and reared in East Point, a suburb of Atlanta. She wrote several poems as a child, and was inspired to begin writing again in 1970. Her work has appeared in several anthology books, including Sparrowgrass Poetry Forum.

In 1999, she established an Internet ministry[*] and now has over 300 poems of inspiration and faith that are touching hearts and lives all over the world.

Today, Connie continues to pen messages in poetry that she believes are divinely inspired. It is her earnest prayer that the biblical truths found in these simple faith messages would touch your heart, enrich your life, and draw you to… a Deeper Faith. ~ To God Be the Glory ~

[*] www.InspirationalPoetry.com & www.ChristianPoems.com

INDEX OF POEMS